Prophetic Justice

Prophetic Justice

Essays and Reflections on
Race, Religion, and Politics

Keith Magee

First published in Great Britain 2020

Published by The Social Justice Institute

Principal: Keith Magee

Editor: Joanne Clay

Cover Design: Obinna Chinemerem Ozuo

Typeset: Obinna Chinemerem Ozuo

British Library Cataloguing-in-Publication Data
Library of Congress Cataloguing-in-Publication Data

Names: Magee, Keith, author.

Title: Prophetic Justice: Essays and Reflections of Race, Religion and Politics / Keith Magee.

Description: London, United Kingdom: Social Justice Institute [2020] | Includes bibliographical references and endnotes.

Identifiers: ISBN 978-1-5272-8330-5 (Hardcover) |
               ISBN 978-1-5272-8354-1 (Paperback) |
               ISBN 979-8-5766-4930-3 (EBook).

Subjects: Social Justice | Race | Religion | Politics | Public Theology | Public Policy | United States of America | African American | Jewish | White America | Prophecy | Social Aspects—United States—Culture—Heritage—History—Socioeconomics.

For more information visit http://www.4JusticeSake.org

*

Herein Is Written

*

To – Zayden, Andre, Holden,

Amauri, Grace and Eleanor

The Lost and the Found

~ with thanksgiving for ~

Karen Pritzker

Barbara Reynolds

Caroline Cracraft

Table of Contents

The Forethought

Since the beginning of time there has been an intersection of belief, values, and religious ideas contributing to the development of societies, cultures, and policies. In a commonly agreed-upon discourse of the Abrahamic religions, Judaism, Christianity, and Islam, the Hebrew prophet Moses is recorded as having been the leader and deliverer of his people from Egyptian slavery. All three major faiths capture the covenant ceremony at Mt. Sinai, where the Ten Commandments were promulgated. These ten public policies and stipulations formed the religious and civil traditions for a community then known as Israel, and still have a significant influence on religious life, moral concerns, and social ethics today.

All around the world, societies and cultures have, nestled within their belief systems, ideologies that impact everyday life and often the rule of law. The Varna caste system in India dominated the Hindu beliefs about how society ought to be structured. The central claim of Nigeria's Yoruba ethnic group is that local and national communicative principles in political discourse should be subsumed under epistemic, ontological, and ethical dimensions drawn from its histories, cultures, and values. In the United Kingdom, the Sovereign holds the title 'Defender of the Faith and Supreme Governor of the Church of England'.

The official motto of the United States of America, 'In God We Trust', places religion firmly at the heart of government. The motto was adopted by the U.S. Congress in 1956, supplanting 'E pluribus unum', the Latin for 'Out of many, one'. Since that time, from the halls of government to the closing stanza of 'The Star-Spangled Banner' and to coins and paper currency, the motto is embedded as a reminder that, come what may, we must keep the faith and put our trust in God.

It is worth noting, however, that the U.S. Constitution itself is a secular document. It only mentions religion twice – once to prevent laws "respecting an establishment of religion or prohibiting the free exercise thereof", and once to prohibit "religious tests" for public office. The Founding Fathers took a clear stance on the separation of Church and state and on the importance of religious freedom for all.

Today in America, as in many developed nations, we are faced with the paradox of the state's supposedly secular nature and its religious underpinnings. American patriotism seems to be tied to the latter in a way that often proves to be divisive rather than uniting. There continues to be a large disconnect as America deals with the issues of culture and society as they intersect with race, religion, and politics. Unlike some nations, America has not brought to bear a revelation from a divine prophet or head of state, leading to a singular, abiding religious system that proclaims the standards of moral codes and policies. Instead, America has heard multiple voices speaking about justice and injustice, morality and immorality, civility and incivility, with many proclaiming that their interpretation and voices speak on behalf of God. I'm of the opinion that we all have room to grow. I for one believe that I'm practising my faith.

It is my efforts to lend my voice within these writings to bring to consideration all that is entangled in America's rhetoric through the lens of race, religion, and politics. Herein lie many things intended to reveal the various dynamics that have brought America to this point. I hope that these writings will enable us to face our fears, both past and present, but, in doing so, also give a sense of real hope and promise for the future.

All the essays included in this book have been written over the course of the last four years. In them, I have sought to capture the stark contrast between the fate of the nation and its soul. Likewise, I explore questions of race and set out how to understand this politically charged construct, while addressing the birthing of racism and its resurgence in the Obama and Trump eras. There is also a description of the kinship of strangers who have both known 'Egypt' – a consideration of the experiences that link Black and Jewish Americans. I examine the bitter-sweet history of slavery, looking at how its complex legacy is now being debated in the public sphere. I try to provide insight into the role and value of Black men in American democracy. Equally, I attempt to place the U.S. Constitution in context and to assert that we should see it as a thread that, if bravely used, can weave a tapestry for all.

I have also included in this collection a series of reflections – these are shorter articles that I've written during the same period, also on the subjects of race, religion, and politics. These include my thoughts on a weeping Jesus and Black Lives Matter; the fact that White poverty is no privilege; the triumph of love over hate; and the truth about the role of Black and White women in our democratic process. I also include an open letter to Vice President Pence that was inspired by prayers with my six-year-old son. I conclude with a prayer for America, a version of which I first shared during a vigil following the murder of George Floyd.

All of this comes from my heart and reflects my training as an economist and public theologian and my roles as an ecumenical minister and social justice seeker and scholar. My thinking is also influenced by my upbringing, as the son of an entrepreneurial craftsman and an award-winning journalist, and by my blended family, which consists of Blacks and Whites, Jews and Jedis, straight people and pansexuals, believers and non-believers. I am – perhaps most importantly – the father of a six-year-old son whose future, along with that of his peers, is the reason why I keep practising my faith and aiming to absorb ever more knowledge about our collective humanity, through research, teaching, and learning.

It is my hope that these seminal writings offer a reflection of the past and give a perspective on the present. They are a call for us to advance towards a place of agreeing that we, together, can frame our future – this is more important now than ever as we set about recovering from the ravages of the Covid-19 pandemic and start to rebuild anew. I hope these words cause you to seek within your being your own prophetic voice. I hope that you will use it to speak truth to power, for that is how we can all be useful within our communities, and especially within a democracy.

I believe that power belongs to God. However, we represent that God – he blesses us with the gifts we need in order to leave behind us something greater than what we inherited. I often say that I hope that my writings represent the voice of God – who becomes voiceless without us.

Keith Magee
London, England
November 2020

CHAPTER ONE

The Fate of a Nation: The Sky Is Falling

"One day Henny Penny was picking up corn in the corn yard when "whack!", something hit her upon the head. 'Goodness gracious me!' said Henny Penny. 'The sky's a-going to fall! I must go and tell the king!'" [1]

Folk tales have significant value in culture and society. They often hold the depth of meaning and traditions. Typically, they are shared through jokes, proverbs, or stories. More often than not, folk tales are passed down through oral traditions, though many are chronicled in bodies of literature. For me, the most memorable of all childhood folk tales is 'Chicken-Little', as it is called in the United States ('Chicken Licken' in the United Kingdom). The resounding phrase that Chicken-Little repeats hysterically as she attempts to make her way to the king is: "The sky is falling!" A simple kernel of corn engenders the mistaken belief that disaster is imminent and that the world is coming to an end.

My faith tradition is rooted in the conservative bayou of Louisiana, in the teachings of the United Methodist Church. In Winan United Methodist Church, a White, blonde-haired, and blue-eyed Jesus Christ was introduced to me as the Lord and Saviour of the world. This Christ, along with his Church, was a place of safety from our personal sins and from the social ills on the outside, yet assuredly also a place of his love. Early in Vacation Bible Study, and later in Sunday School, we were taught "Yes, Jesus loves me", along with all the principles of Christianity through simplified stories. The Book of Discipline provided us with the doctrine, guiding principles, and tenants of our belief. The Holy Bible's objective was to bring us closer to the understanding of the love of the Lord, Jesus Christ, through his life, death, and resurrection. The most glaring and fundamental lesson of all was that his resurrection and ascension place us in the 'end times'. Someday soon, the Lord would come back to receive those who believed 'on him'. It was a stark message to teach children – that this loving God's son would be coming any day now and that our dreams of growing up and having lives filled with earthly promises might not be realized.

In the Biblical literature of Matthew's Gospel, the 24th chapter predicts the destruction of the Temple and describes the signs that would identify the coming of the end times through the prophetic words of the Jew from Nazareth, Jesus. He is sitting on the Mount of Olives and the disciples come to him for a private conversation about his imminent departure. They ask him: "What will be the sign of your coming and of the end of the age?" In the narrative that Jesus gives in reply, he says specifically:

> *"You will hear of wars and rumours of wars, but see to it that you are not alarmed. Such things must happen, but the end is still to come. Nation will rise against nation, and kingdom against kingdom. There will be famines and earthquakes in various places."* [2]

The word nation is translated from 'ethnos', which is the root of 'ethnicity'. [3] For centuries, we have seen ethnic groups at war with each other. In America, there has been the imposition of an ethnic and racial hierarchy. Embedded in religious teachings, this hierarchy has been a part of American culture for over four hundred years, since the first colonizers landed in Jamestown, Virginia, in 1607.

In the same period, other White settlers, now known as Pilgrims, arrived in Cape Cod, Massachusetts in 1620. They had fled England, where they were persecuted for their separatist religious beliefs. The Church of England had been established in 1534 by King Henry VIII who declared himself its head. Although both Henry VIII and his daughter, Queen Elizabeth I, had sought to differentiate it from the Roman Catholic Church, some Christians felt that the Church of England's practices were still too mired in those of the old church. These radicals became known as 'Puritans' because they sought to purify the church, calling for simpler, less structured forms of worship.

These two notable groups of early American colonizers needed individuals to work the land, till the soil, and serve their needs. The first of these slave labourers would be their former allies, the Native Americans, who had taught the newly arrived Europeans how to survive and harvest the land. Soon to become more prominent were imported African slaves, who had been kidnapped, bound and sold into slavery with the sanction of "the Church".

Many of the African slaves who survived the horrors of the Middle Passage and reached America would find kinship, hope, and faith in the notion of Christ, the suffering servant. They came to believe that suffering with him might make it possible to reign with him in eternity. This Jesus aligned with many of the slaves' native traditions of worshipping an ancestor who had power over death. They believed that their own bloody sacrifice could be redeeming, and that communing with the spirit of Christ would help them to bear their pain. After all, Jesus, through his Hebrew linage, was descended from a people who had themselves been enslaved by a pharaoh and had once lived in bondage. Yet, there remained a pervasive and stark difference between Jesus and the slaves. Depictions of Christ represented pure whiteness. His skin and even his blood – which, once shed on the cross, could "wash clean" – were "as white as snow".

Even more daunting was the fact that the same symbol of the cross of salvation was burned by White supremacists as a form of intimidation. Such acts were intended to remind Black people that even this White saviour couldn't rescue them from the venom of hate and incivility. In 1915 William J. Simmons, a United Methodist itinerant minister, instigated the second incarnation of the Klu Klux Klan. In an act meant to consecrate the Klan's Christian morality, the founding ceremony included setting a cross afire atop of Stone Mountain, Georgia.[4] The burning cross would become a powerful Klan symbol. A song entitled 'The Bright Fiery Cross' even became their anthem, although it had originally been written as a hymn by the Methodist preacher, Reverend George Bennard in 1912. Troubled with despair as he evangelized, Bennard had begun to meditate upon the vital importance of the cross, as being inseparable from saving grace. His hymn, called 'The Old Rugged Cross', was popularized by the Evangelist Bill Sunday, but the words were then adapted for the Klan by Alvia O. Dree as 'The Bright Fiery Cross. Our Song':

> "To the bright fiery cross, I will ever be true;
> All blame and reproach gladly bear;
> And friendship will show to each Klansman I know;
> Its glory forever we'll share."

Chorus:

"So, I'll cherish the Bright Fiery Cross;

Till from duties at last I lay down.

Then burn o'er me a Bright Fiery Cross;

The day I am laid in the ground."[5]

The duality of religion and the vulnerability of Black lives was something I learned long ago from my father, who was a lover of dogs. As he would sit out back on a stump, he would give me world wisdoms. He often told me that "if you keep kicking a dog, he will bite back". Yet, within Christian teaching, the preaching of "whosoever shall smite thee on thy right cheek, turn to him the other also" seemed to apply only to Black people, while some White Christians raged injustice and violence against Black communities and their leaders.

Just over 50 years ago, in 1968, the Klu Klux Klan offered a $100,000 bounty for the assassination of the non-violent Civil Rights leader Reverend Dr. Martin Luther King, Jr., resulting in his cowardly shooting by James Earl Ray.[6] However, in 2009, just before the 40th anniversary of Dr. King's death, America would inaugurate its first African American President, Barack Obama. This moment caused many African Americans to pause and to believe that perhaps there was a glimmer of hope that the suffering servant would not have to wait until after the end times to have a bit of heaven on earth.

As a senior religious affairs advisor to the Obama presidential campaign, I witnessed first-hand African American faith leaders declaring that Barack Obama had been sent by God. In July 2008, during the Quadrennial Session of the African Methodist Episcopal (the church Richard Allen and Absalom Jones founded after being dragged out of a Methodist church in 1787[7]), the leadership laid hands on and offered prayers over Obama – an act of impartation in the lexicon of Black Christianity.[8] During the campaign in Colorado, a Black man brandishing an Obama placard marched back and forth in a state of feverish excitement, shouting: "He's been sent by God! I'm not saying he's Jesus, but he could fill Moses' shoes!"

There is a distinct difference between a prophet and a president. Theologian, scholar, and pastor Marvin McMickle contends in his 2006 book Where Have All

The Prophets Gone? Reclaiming Prophetic Preaching in America that prophets preached truth to power. They did so, he writes, to the point of having to attack monarchs and the ruling elite, who put more confidence in armies and alliances than they did in the God who had brought them into that land:

> *"With an urgency that could not be contained and a fervor that could not be controlled, the prophets declared their 'Thus says the Lord', despite the ridicule, rebuke, and outright rejection that most of them experienced throughout their lives."* [9]

Early in the campaign, Obama was forced to address the issue of race following the emergence of a YouTube clip showing excerpts from sermons by his prophetic Chicago pastor, the Reverend Jeremiah Wright. The Obamas had attended Trinity United Church of Christ for over 20 years; Wright had officiated at their wedding there. In the clip, aggressively aired by the media, Wright was seen fulminating that Blacks should not sing 'God Bless America' but 'God Damn America'. He referred to the country as the "U-S-K-K-K-of-A" and said that the United States had brought on the 9/11 attacks with its own "terrorism" policy. [10]

The controversy heightened after Wright gave a speech at the National Press Club in April, 2008, in which he declared that:

> "The prophetic theology of the Black church is not only a theology of liberation; it is also a theology of transformation, which is also rooted in Isaiah 61, the text from which Jesus preached in his inaugural message as recorded by Luke. When you read the entire passage from either Isaiah 61 or Luke 4, and do not try to understand the passage or the content of the passage in the context of a sound bite, what you see is God's desire for a radical change in a social order that has gone sour."

In the midst of the controversy brewing over Wright's stance, Obama delivered what would be his landmark speech on race. In it he acknowledged White fears and Black resentments. He spoke of "the complexities of race in this country that we've never really worked through – a part of our union that we have yet to perfect." The fact that so many had been surprised to hear the anger in Wright's sermons, he went on, "simply reminds us of the old truism that the most segregated hour in American life occurs on Sunday morning." But the "profound mistake" that Wright had made, Obama said, was not to speak about racism in America. "It's that he spoke as if our society was static; as if no progress has been made; as if this country – a country that has made it possible for one of his own members to run for the highest office in the land and build a coalition of White and Black, Latino and Asian, rich and poor, young and old – is still irrevocably bound to a tragic past. But what we know – what we have seen – is that America can change. That is the true genius of this nation."[11]

Though Obama was able to win a second term in 2012, there were many White Americans who remained outraged at having a Black president. Their anger was deeply embedded with the idea that White privilege was unravelling before their very eyes. However, in 2007 in Ohio, I'd met several working-class and working-poor White men and women who were committed to supporting Obama. The recurring message from them was that they believed that "a Black man will understand what it means to be poor and want to take care of your family".[12] And while that would, seemingly, be the aim of Obama's policies – from the Affordable Health Care Act to the automotive-industry bailout, from the Environment Protection Agency's emissions standards to the United States Department of Education's Pell Grants – this didn't translate into jobs or a safety net. No benefit was immediately felt in the pockets of most Americans, let alone poor and working-class Whites. As they watched Blacks being celebrated in Washington, these White Americans were starting to feel that this 'Black messiah' deemed them to be unimportant.

By the end of Obama's second term there was also silent outrage and discontent within many poor and working-class African American communities at what appeared to have been the failures of America's first Black president. Many had bought into the idea of a prophetic voice, with a messianic message, that would create overt opportunities of equality and, perhaps, reparation. The notion of 'the chosen one' was unravelling, because the message no longer felt prophetic, and many Black people were realizing that presidents aren't prophets and certainly not messiahs or magicians.

The emergence of Donald Trump as the GOP nominee for the 2016 election seemed to offer a sense of hope for both marginalized Whites, who felt left behind, and wealthy Americans, who wanted tax protections. Trump's message was simple: "Make America great again!".[13] This was code for: "Make America White again!" He had already begun fanning the flames of discord as the driving force of the 'birther movement' questioning President Obama's legitimacy. After being inaugurated as the 45th President of the United States and taking occupancy in the White House in January 2017, President Trump continued this venom by calling Mexicans rapists and targeting Muslims with a travel ban. What was even more jarring was that the White Evangelical church aligned in support of President Trump's agenda to 'save' America from the supposed sins of the liberal left, notably through his promise to protect religious rights through judicial appointments.

The Grand Ole Party – which once opposed the expansion of slavery and then, with the election of Abraham Lincoln, led its abolition, attracting many African American voters – gravely shifted after the Civil Rights Act of 1964 and the Voting Rights Act of 1965. Whites from southern states in which White supremacists proclaimed the virtues of Jim Crow laws became the Republican Party's core voters. The U.S. Supreme Court's 1973 decision to protect abortion rights in Roe v. Wade created a new party platform, growing Republican support among 'pro-life' Evangelicals. In 2016, it would be White Evangelicals who would vote at a rate of 81% for Trump.[14]

White supremacy theology has always been, and remains, hostile towards non-Whites, in particular towards Black men. In August 2018, while meeting with Evangelical Christian leaders, President Trump told them that there would be "violence" if Republicans lost their majority in Congress as a result of the November mid-term elections. He told them to take to their pulpits to tell their followers that this was a referendum on him, their religion, and freedom of speech. The same religion that tells Black people "be patient; love thy neighbour; honour thy mother and father; don't steal, cheat, or commit adultery" seemed to use 'white-out' to affirm President Trump. A self-confessed adulterer, a man who pays for sex (prostitution) and speaks freely about being able to walk down 5th Avenue and shoot someone, was being touted as the one to save and make America great again.

Within President Trump's administration, it could be argued that White supremacy reigns within the White House, under the leadership of an Imperial Wizard, the self-declared King. In this simple yet daunting analogy, the Republican Party is serving as the Klexter – the outer-guard protecting its King. The right-leaning U.S. Supreme Court is the Klarogo – the sergeant-at-arms – yielding the rule of law to its King. The public-facing reality of the Klan mentality proves to be alive and well.

This hatred under the guise of religious teachings can no longer be met with patience, peace talks, or Twitter protests. And it certainly can't be met with preaching the Gospel of Jesus's love to a Christian sect which apparently embraces the Klan. Nor can any hope lie in America's President, Donald Trump, who affirmed to his Texas supporters that he's a "proud nationalist".[15] He only continues to ignite more flames that threaten to engulf our sacred symbols. Yet, we must not passively resign ourselves to accepting that such is our fate.

Fate is believed to be a power that causes and controls all events, leaving us powerless to change or influence the way things will happen. The fear of an impending sudden or drawn-out end is critical to the notion of fate. This fear has no doubt always been with us. The tale of Henny Penny first appeared at least 25 centuries ago in the Buddhist scriptures as the 'Daddabha Jataka' ('The Sound of the Hare').[16] Upon hearing about some particular religious practices, the prophet, the Buddha, explains that there is no special merit in them, but rather that they are "like the noise the hare heard". He then tells the story of a hare disturbed by a falling fruit who believes that the world is coming to an end. The hare starts a stampede among the other animals until a lion halts them, investigates the cause of the panic, and restores calm. The fable teaches the necessity for deductive reasoning and subsequent investigation.

The games company Delightworks has an online role-playing mobile game called 'Fate/Grand Order'.[17] The game involves turn-based combat in which the player, who takes on the role of a 'Master', summons and commands powerful familiars known as 'Servants' to battle against enemies. The plot centres on the Chaldea Security Organization's discovery that the eradication of humankind is imminent. A grand order to fight fate is issued: two heroes must travel back in time to learn how to save humanity by changing the past and thus restoring the future.

The unfortunate use of religion since the beginning of the ages to stoke racial strife and violence remains prevalent in societies. However, just as in Fate/Grand Order, we the players have the capacity to determine who wins or loses and the ability to avert disaster for ourselves. The underpinning of the hatred spread by the Ku Klux Klan and a deeply seeded Evangelical White supremacy theology, coupled with the suffocating to death of Black lives by those in a blue uniform, are causing a racial outrage in America. White Evangelicals are invoking the theology of end times, using the Bible to justify their actions, while also trying to subjugate Black people in the name of that same God.

The White Evangelical prosperity preacher and pastor, Paula White, spiritual advisor to President Trump, issued a fiery message on January 5, 2020. She addressed her rebuke to the "strange wind" that was sent to hurt the church, sent against President Trump, and sent against her. She is clear in her stance and in her belief in the name and blood of Jesus, decreeing:

> *"We break it by the superior blood of Jesus right now. In the name of Jesus, we command all Satanic pregnancies to miscarry right now."* [18]

The Black church and its preachers aren't uttering much. So, that can't be the "strange wind". McMickle's inquiry of the Black prophetic voice, that brought justice to its people, was done with Black prophetic preachers, who understand the radical Jewish son of God who was committed to justice and equality. What was regrettably omitted from the media's reporting of Reverend Wright's April 2008 address were the prophetic words that he spoke to heal America – words about our progress as opposed to where we'd come from. Wright was clear that God doesn't desire for us, as his children, to be at war with each other. He was clear that God doesn't want us to see each other as superior or inferior, to hate each other, abuse each other, misuse each other, define each other, or put each other down. The Prophet (Wright) said:

> *"God wants us reconciled one to another, and that third principle in the prophetic theology of the Black church is also and has*

always been at the heart of the Black church experience in North America. When Richard Allen and Absalom Jones were dragged out of St. George's Methodist Episcopal Church in Philadelphia during the same year, 1787, when the Constitution was framed in Philadelphia, for daring to kneel at their altar next to White worshipers, they founded the Free African Society, and they welcomed White members into their congregation to show that reconciliation was the goal, not retaliation. " [19]

The fate of our nation could lead to war, but that doesn't have to be the case if all of the players understand the necessity for deductive reasoning and subsequent investigation, and address America's 400 years of a conscious race problem. Could the kernel of corn be more about awakening a nation to truly believe in the God of love and justice, in whom it says it trusts, rather than foretelling a destructive end?

CHAPTER TWO

It's Called Race: Towards a Collective Humanity

"Suppose someone is superior in playing the flute but much inferior in birth or in good looks, then, even granting that each of these things – birth and beauty – is a greater good than the ability to play the flute, and even though they surpass flute-playing proportionately more than the best flute-player surpasses the others in flute-playing, even so the best flute-player ought to be given the outstandingly good flutes." [1] *– Aristotle*

Michael Sandel is the Anne T. and Robert M. Bass Professor of Government at Harvard University. He teaches a course on Justice in which he poses the question: "What is the right thing to do?"[2] He invokes Aristotle's conception of morality to examine this element that is often missing from existing democratic debate. Sandel asks the audience the same question Aristotle posed some 2,300 years ago: "Suppose we are giving out flutes. Who should get the best ones?" Audience members tend to give one of three answers: the best players, the worst players, and/or random citizens.[3]

Aristotle sided with the best players, asserting that flutes are meant to be played well, that is their purpose. Sandel argues that when we are making such decisions – about how to fairly distribute objects, wealth, opportunities, or even justice itself – we have to consider not only the purpose of a thing, but also the qualities in it that are worth honouring. He says:

> "There is a tendency to think that if we engage too directly with moral questions that we create a recipe for disagreement, and for that matter, a recipe for intolerance and coercion."

Sandel concludes:

> "It seems to me that ... a better way to have mutual respect is to engage directly with the

moral convictions 'citizens' bring to public life, rather than to require that people leave their deepest moral convictions outside before they enter." [4]

In order to explore race, it is essential that we create spaces of reasoning and investigating, conviction, and change. What is happening prominently in America now is the increasingly visible proliferation of Black and Brown bodies being murdered, predominately by White men. As a result, the Black Lives Matter movement[5] has taken the world by storm. There is now civil unrest all around the world because of this thing called race – and a hashtag created by a group of people in a moment of fear and anger has now become a rallying cry. All because of this thing called race.

The concept of race was devised as a classification of human beings with the purpose of giving power and legitimacy to White people over non-White people. Race is a political construct, invented by people, not a natural development. The entire construct of race then, is a false classification of people, that isn't based on any real or accurate biological or scientific truth. Whereas race is a false construct, ethnicity is not.

Ethnicity is solid as a connector of particular groups of people who share some common ancestry, traditions, language, or dialect.

I am of the opinion – and I believe I have evidence for this – that race can be deconstructed in the next four generations. However, it will take courage and a belief in our collective humanity to overcome centuries of theories that have divided us.

The term 'White' emerged as a classification during the 1700s in the British colonies of North America where it served to unite European settlers and increase their dominance over the Native Americans and African slaves. For those who could identify as 'White', the label would prove hugely valuable for centuries to come and the repercussions of the racial divide it created would be felt around the globe. In Paul Kivel's work Uprooting Racism: How White People Can Work for Racial Justice, he asserts that: "Whiteness is a constantly shifting boundary separating those who are entitled to have certain privileges from those whose exploitation and vulnerability to violence is justified by their not being white."[6]

There are four key factors that have constructed race and therefore created this racial divide: religion, social science, medicine, and eugenics.

During the Reformation, in the sixteenth and seventeenth centuries, Christian religious leaders debated whether Blacks and 'Indians' (as they called the indigenous people of North and South America) were human. As slavery grew increasingly profitable, racism became an economic necessity and religion was used as a means to justify it by classifying people of colour as 'pagan and soulless'. However, religious justifications became more difficult to sustain as large numbers of people of colour were converted to Christianity. New justifications were required to explain the differences between people in ways that could be used to assert the supposed superiority of Whites.

In 1859 the English naturalist, geologist, and biologist Charles Darwin published On the Origin of Species, in which he outlined his theory of evolution and described the concept of 'the survival of the fittest'. Although there was nothing inherently racist in Darwin's theory, others quickly exploited it to excuse racism and even genocide. In 1864, W. Winwood Reade, a British explorer who described himself as a "disciple of Darwin", concluded his book Savage Africa with a stark prediction on the future of the Black race: "England and France will rule Africa. Africans will dig the ditches and water the deserts. It will be hard work and the Africans will probably become extinct. We must learn to look at the result with composure. It illustrates the beneficent law of nature, that the weak must be devoured by the strong."[7]

In the eighteenth and nineteenth centuries, pseudoscience came up with a range of terms to explain racial differences. These included 'Mongoloid' and 'Caucazoid', both of which have linguistic roots referring to geographic areas, and 'Negroid', which refers to colour alone. Multiple medical 'studies', supported by research that we now know to have had no scientific basis, disseminated the myth that people of colour were intellectually inferior. These false theories led to the emergence of eugenics – the idea that the human population could be improved by increasing the reproduction of people judged to have 'superior' genes while preventing that of those with 'inferior' genes. Hugely popular in the United

States in the early twentieth century, eugenics would be adopted by the Nazi regime in Germany with tragic consequences.

The whole invalid concept of race is based on merely on the colour of a human being's skin. I believe that this thing called race equates to a horrible skin disease. However, there is a cure.

The skin is the body's largest organ. It protects us from microbes and the elements, helps regulate body temperature, and permits the sensations of touch, heat, and cold. We have three layers of skin. The epidermis, the outermost layer, provides a waterproof barrier and creates our skin tone. The dermis, beneath the epidermis, contains tough connective tissue, hair follicles, and sweat glands. The deeper subcutaneous tissue, or hypodermis, is made of fat and connective tissue.[8]

The skin's colour thus appears only on the outermost layer, but has become a defining agent. We've spent generations living with a false narrative of race because of an external layer. That false narrative has given cause to deeply embedded hate, venom, bigotry, racism, violence, and death. That's why the late Reverend Dr.

Martin Luther King, Jr. dreamed of a day when non-White children "would not be judged by the colour of their skin but by the content of their character".[9]

Within our character is where we find our souls. Greek philosophers, such as Aristotle, Plato, and Socrates, understood that the soul must have a logical faculty, the exercise of which was the most divine of human actions. At his trial, Socrates even summarized his teaching as nothing other than an exhortation for his fellow Athenians to excel in matters of the psyche, "since all bodily goods are dependent on such excellence".[10]

In Judaism and in Christianity, only human beings have immortal souls (although immortality is disputed within Judaism and the concept of immortality may have been influenced by Plato[11]). The Biblical literature in Genesis 2 says that God formed man (humankind) "from the dust of the ground and breathed into his nostrils the breath of life".[12] The breath of God then causes man to become a living soul.

Rather than exploring the colour of skins, I'd rather that we consider, in brave spaces, the colour of our souls – looking beyond the exterior into our collective humanity. With the continuing murders of Black and Brown bodies necessitating the need to declare that "Black Lives Matter", I believe it's time to explore how the identity of the 'soul' extends far beyond the pervasive false construct of race. I mean the soul as it is defined by many religious, philosophical, and mythological traditions – as the moral being, the inner yearning, and the quest for good. The soul as the ethereal essence of a living being.

I'm by no means offering a pass to the perpetuators of acts of terrorism. I believe that we must gather White men, first, to allow them to analyze race, culture, and systemic White privilege,[13] and other social phenomena generated by the societal compositions, perceptions, and group behaviours of White people in relation to the soul. Then, we should build on this knowledge to embrace a collective humanity – so that no one is deemed sub-human and without a soul.

It will take generations. I understand the urgency of now, but we can't fool ourselves into thinking that we can dismantle systemic racism, which is so embedded in societal norms, through mass protest alone. It will take more than toppling statues, rolling them through city streets until they are in harbours, or having a few family members and friends who are the other, and thereby believing that we are different. None of that will suffice, because there's something that must be redeemed in our souls.

Nor can we believe that racism can be overcome by laws alone. We look to the American Civil Rights movement as a model. And yet, we often miss the most important element of the movement. The Civil Rights Act of 1964 and other laws were created because there was an uncivil group of people – White people – who needed laws to make them civil.[14] Those laws were enforced to protect Black people because they had been deemed not to have a soul. If those laws had worked, we wouldn't be declaring that Black Lives Matter today.

As an academic I have the pleasure of teaching social justice and the Civil Rights movement. I have found that within the halls of universities we have the opportunity to awaken and enlighten beautiful and curious minds with deeper meaning. It is believed that in the universe of higher education you are exposed to research that is taught so that a student may learn and discern the truth. Many of the great American universities take this to heart. The University of

Pennsylvania, Harvard, and Yale have embedded in their seals the Latin word Veritas. In Roman mythology Veritas is the goddess of truth. These are places where academics and students alike are activated within their various disciplines to disrupt the normative, because together they are on the 'Veritas', the quest for truth. Is it not through informed education, that investigates and challenges the construct of race, that we can bring to light the truths of our collective humanity and therefore can change the world – one generation at a time?

CHAPTER THREE

Birthing Racism: An Invisible Empire

*"I, the undersigned, a true and loyal citizen
of the United States of America, being a
white woman of sound mind and a believer
in the tenets of the Christian religion and
the principles of 'pure Americanism', do most
respectfully apply for affiliation in the Ladies
of the Invisible Empire." – from 'Women
Klan Members Reveal Family Life'* [1]

Movies have the ability to bring us out of our everyday reality and to take us into places of fiction and nonfiction, to entertain us, and even awaken unconsciousness. My all-time favourite movie is African American female director Kasi Lemmons' 1997 Eve's Bayou set in our nation's Deep South.[2] Louisiana bayous are strange and wonderful places – a world unto their own, overflowing with a wealth of stories and thematic possibilities. At the start of the film, Lemmons introduces us to the area's enigmatic nature, beginning with a declaration: "Memory is a selection of images, some elusive, others printed indelibly on the brain."

One century after The Birth of a Nation premiered, with its explicit stereotypes and embedded hatred of Black Americans, America began deeply grappling with its seemingly indelible racism. A nation that had appeared to make progress in the election of Barack Obama, its first President of both African-Kenyan and White American heritage, began to relive painful memories. Rather than being fully conscious of her (America's) progress, she began a travailing in re-birth. Arguably, the 'birther' inquisition, led by the then GOP presidential nominee Donald Trump, gave credence to this resurgence. Trump's questioning of President Obama's legitimacy and identity wasn't actually based in concern about whether Obama was born in America. It spoke to an inherent privilege to determine if, where, how, and to whom one belonged. America has never fully grappled with its gritty memory and now, again, its sobering present.

In 1915, President Woodrow Wilson hosted a special White House screening of D.W. Griffith's The Birth of a Nation. Based on The Clansman, written by Wilson's friend Thomas Dixon,[3] the film was a racial marker of the time. It portrayed Black politicians as drunken buffoons and set the stage for the Ku Klux Klan's savage attempts to remove them from office. You would think that showing such a film would spark outrage today. That is now questionable. However, its original White House screening really shouldn't surprise us, given President Wilson's track record at the time of segregating federal workers[4] in Washington, D.C. After the end of World War I, Wilson would block efforts to include racial equality as a founding principle of the League of Nations.

In the early 1920s the Ku Klux Klan, defunct since the 1870s, was revived and began a new crusade for a White, native-born, Protestant America. During this second phase, Klan membership grew dramatically in small towns and rural areas in the north, midwest, and west as well as in the south. In just over ten years, an estimated three to six million people joined the movement.

Across the country, female auxiliaries played a key supportive role in the successful rebirth of the Klan through the Women of the Klu Klux Klan (WKKK), which was given its own charter in 1923. Many of the women who joined were the daughters, sisters, and wives of Klansmen and wanted to contribute to the Klan cause and promote family togetherness.

The WKKK primarily interpreted the struggle for women's voting rights through the lens of class, ethnic, and racial privilege. They existed in parallel, in some respects, to the wider women's suffrage movement, and embodied White supremacy, nativist, and racist politics. Some of the key motivating factors for members of the WKKK included their opposition to immigration, racial equality, Jewish-owned businesses, and parochial schools. They fuelled the notion that America was experiencing serious moral decay.

In a blatant falsification of the Reconstruction period, Birth of a Nation presented Black men as dominating Southern Whites and, in particular, as using sexual force on White women. This became a pervasive concern for the WKKK. They felt a need to protect themselves and preserve their womanhood.

The ideology of womanhood, for these women, was aligned with early feminism.[5] Feminism was first introduced at the beginning of the 1900s as women were slowly mobilizing for equal rights. These rights were crucial if women were to become part of the political landscape. With a steady hand, White women would gain the rights to own land and to vote. During World War II, women were in the workplace as the majority of men were fighting on the front lines. Many women found themselves working as skilled labourers in factories to keep the country running. By the time their male counterparts, and even fathers, brothers, and sons, returned at the end of the war years, women had found a new identity and did not want to give up their jobs and freedoms. And, yet, many maintained their sense of womanhood by keeping their homes well-stocked with food, in case war broke out again, and with ammunition, for fighting any necessary battles.

Their quest for equality with White men would not prohibit many White women from joining the Klan's ranks to protect their families. A 1923 advertisement recruited women for the WKKK using 'American' rights and 'pure womanhood' as code words for racial and national privilege:

> "*To the American Women of Washington: Are you interested in the welfare of our Nation? As an enfranchised woman are you interested in Better Government? Do you not wish for the protection of Pure Womanhood? Shall we uphold the sanctity of the American Home? Should we not interest ourselves in Better Education for our children? Do we not want American teachers in our American schools? IT IS POSSIBLE FOR ORGANIZED PATRIOTIC WOMEN TO AID IN STAMPING OUT THE CRIME AND VICE THAT ARE UNDERMINING THE MORALS OF OUR YOUTH. The duty of the American Mother is greater than ever before.*" [6]

One of the commonly held myths surrounding White supremacists is that they are ignorant and uneducated. Nothing could have been further from the truth. Both the male and female Klan members were often highly respected in their communities.

Many of the White women in the WKKK were trained and skilled as teachers, nurses, shop owners, and ordained ministers. The common denominator for women was church affiliation, which included Baptists, Methodists, and Quakers.

The identity of God, as seen through the prism of American Protestantism's whiteness, has been embedded in White women since the founding of America. In Constantino Brumidi's fresco 'The Apotheosis of Washington', in the eye of the Rotunda of the U.S. Capitol, the goddesses of Victory and Liberty appear, along with 13 White maidens who represent America's original colonies. It is of note that George Washington is duly elevated to the status of a god. [7]Brumidi's painting has been interpreted as a true depiction by many who simply take it at face value, denoting that White women have both a celestial place in God and within the halls of government.

Central to Protestantism is the French reformer John Calvin[8] and his theory that only a select few are predestined for salvation from birth. White American Protestants believed that they were God's chosen few, especially when they had wealth. All non-White Americans, they thought, could be granted salvation through the extension of grace. One of the fundamental ways to access this grace was by doing the hard work of creating God's kingdom on earth through a secular vocation. If you didn't enjoy measurable, tangible success it was believed that you had been denied God's grace. In this context, Blacks could be blamed for their own plight and therefore could be seen as needing to work to obtain the salvation that was automatically gifted to White Americans.

Within this essential belief system, the native-born, Protestant Women of the Klu Klux Klan are inferior to White men, but superior to Blacks. Women's Suffrage movement leader Susan B. Anthony was brought up in a Quaker family with a long activist tradition. Early in her life she developed a sense of justice and moral zeal and, yet, she stated:

> *"I will cut off this right arm of mine before I will ever work or demand the ballot for the Negro and not the woman."* [9]

Daisy Douglas Brushwiller was also from a devout Quaker family. At the age of four she first felt inspired to testify to her spiritual commitment. At eight years old and again at twelve she felt "a personal call from

God" to preach and spread the Gospel. She became a sought after 'girl evangelist' and later became a pastor of the Muncie, Indiana, Quaker meeting. Before taking on her pastoral role, she married a schoolteacher, Thomas Barr. It was at her urging that he joined the KKK.[10]

In 1923, while preaching the Gospel in Asheville, North Carolina, Daisy Barr, as she now was, attended a KKK rally. She approached the podium, hushing a crowd of men. She began to read a poem:

> *"I am clothed with wisdom's mantle ... I am strong beyond my years; My hand typifies strength, And, although untrained in cunning, Its movements mark the quaking of the enemies of my country. My eye, though covered, is all-seeing; It penetrates the dark recesses of law violation, Treason, political corruption, and injustice, Causing these cowardly culprits to bare their unholy faces ... My feet are swift to carry the strength of my hand And the penetrations of my all-seeing eye. My nature is serious, righteous, and just, And tempered with the love of Christ.*

> *My purpose is noble, far-reaching, and age-*
> *lasting ... I am the Spirit of Righteousness.*
> *They call me the Ku Klux Klan. I am more*
> *than the uncouth robe and hood; With which*
> *I am clothed. YEA, I AM THE SOUL OF*
> *AMERICA.* " [11]

As this oration demonstrates, Barr is known for having been as steadfast a cheerleader for White supremacy as she was for women's rights, arguing that "no nation rises above its womanhood" and stating her "disgust" at the increasing number of immigrants coming to the country.[12] Barr would become the Imperial Empress of a women's Klan affiliate, Queens of the Golden Mask. She would amass enormous power within the KKK and, along, with many other White Protestant women, would remain intent on marginalizing Blacks. The long history of White women asserting their fear of Black people, getting cops to arrest them and, in some cases, causing their death, is riveting. Is the danger that they are feeling connected to losing their place within the White patriarchy?

There are haunting instances of White women's actions leading to a Black person's death. In 1955 a devout White Christian woman, Carolyn Bryant of Money, Mississippi, accused a 14-year-old boy of following her behind the counter of the store she co-owned, grabbing her waist, and bragging that he'd had sexual encounters with White women. That evening her husband and brother-in-law found Emmitt Till at his relative's home. That night they lynched him and threw his body into the Tallahatchie River. Till's death is one of the pivotal moments in the Civil Rights movement. It would not be until 50 years later that Bryant would confess to having lied.

In the film, The Color Purple, based on Alice Walker's 1982 Pulitzer-winning novel set in 1930s-era rural Georgia, one scene provides a fictional yet typical portrayal of a privileged White woman. The town mayor's wife, Miss Millie (played by Dana Ivey) walks up to Sofia (played by Oprah Winfrey), a Black woman, and is overwhelmed by the cleanliness of her children. She proceeds to ask Sofia if she would like to become her maid. Sofia's heartfelt refusal results in the mayor beating her unconscious with the butt of his pistol. Sofia is imprisoned and later released to work as Miss Millie's maid.

Alice Walker first used the term 'womanist' in 'Coming Apart', a short story she wrote in 1979.[13]

Walker defined a 'womanist' as a "Black feminist or feminist of color. From the Black expression of mothers to female children, 'You acting womanish'", referring to grown-up behaviour.[14] Walker further explains that a womanist is also:

> "A woman who loves other women, sexually and/or nonsexually. Appreciates and prefers women's culture, women's emotional flexibility ... and women's strength. ... Committed to survival and wholeness of entire people, male and female. Not a separatist, except periodically, for health ... Loves music. Loves dance. Loves the moon. Loves the Spirit ... Loves struggle. Loves the folk. Loves herself. Regardless. Womanist is to feminist as purple is to lavender."[15]

The fundamental difference between womanism and feminism ideology is whom each one is rallying against. Feminists are fighting White male patriarchy and the stigmatisms that exist against women. Womanists are fighting discrimination in terms of their race and colour. Both hold family wellness to be central, although, historically, the White woman saw her religion and race as the sources of her superiority.

Just months before Mr. Trump would become U.S. President, the film director and actor Nate Parker reclaimed the Birth of a Nation title. He repurposed it, from its original role as a propaganda tool to falsely depict Black men as rapists and murderers of White women, to a vehicle to challenge racism and White supremacy in America.[16] Parker depicted the same issues that were shown in the original film, but from a different vantage point. Parker chooses the slave-rebellion leader Nat Turner as his central character. When Turner's master positions him as a preacher to his fellow slaves – and makes money from the preaching engagements – Turner begins to see the scope of slavery. The system's consequences are pervasive and reach further than he'd fully imagined. In a riveting scene, Turner rouses his fellow enslaved faith community with a call towards justice. He empowers them as the individuals creating America's prominence and wealth, and thereby deserving of equality.

As film director Lemmons reminded us: "Memory is a selection of images, some elusive, others printed indelibly on the brain." There is great danger, however, when false memories bring to bear misinformation and misattribution. Some White women have held false memories about Black men being predators and rapists, and have handed these false memories down to their offspring. In doing so, they have been responsible for the taking of innocent lives as opposed to birthing life, and for creating fear rather than stimulating love.

A friend shared with me the memory of giving birth to her first child. Beyond the agony of labour, she said that it brings something "new" into the world that you commit to nurture and protect. It is also a time of bringing two families together as one. But, that was her memory of the birth process, after the 36 weeks of the child becoming in her womb.

Memory becomes distinct to who we are, both the good and the bad. It gives us the capability to learn to cherish that which is rewarding and to adapt from those recollections which can hold us hostage to unsavoury experiences. Memory is the storage of our journey and its evidence manifests in our behaviours, within our recall and our ability to recognize. When memory is fully informed it can become a place to reflect and learn, to grow and evolve, bringing about meaning and, when necessary, change.

Our nation is again in an abyss. Beyond Russian interference, we have data that provides evidence that 53% of White women were in full support of Donald Trump and remain firmly in his base. Are we witnessing a resurgence of the White women's invisible empire? Have they re-emerged to rebirth America's racism? When we look to the Trump administration's economics, to social policies, to leadership of the Supreme Court, White women had the ability to change the narrative on all these things and yet they didn't. How do they reconcile themselves with an American President who makes lude comments about "grabbing them by the pussy", committing adultery, or paying to sleep with porn stars? Have their long-held values of womanhood blinded them from seeing their own marginalization?

In June 2019, I met nurse Ellen while in the emergency room in Wellington, Florida. She's a 64-year old White, Protestant President Trump supporter. She enquired as to why I was in Wellington. I shared that I was writing a book on race, religion, and politics in the Obama and Trump eras. It led us to talking politics.

The most jarring part of our discussion was about the content of an interview that President Trump had given to ABC News' George Stephanopoulos in the Oval Office just a few days earlier. Stephanopoulos had asked the President whether his campaign would accept information about his Democratic rival from foreign powers – such as China or Russia – or hand it over the FBI. Ellen was insistent that President Trump did not reply: "I think maybe you do both. I think you might want to listen, there isn't anything wrong with listening. If somebody called from a country, [say] Norway, [and said] 'we have information on your opponent' – oh, I think I'd want to hear it."[17]

I asked Ellen whether she thought President Trump had violated the U.S. Constitution and election laws. Her response was, "Did Hillary?" I then asked her why she was deflecting to Hillary, rather than answering my question. She became horribly upset, saying: "People should stop lying about my President. If he would have said it, I would know!" I suggested that she Google it.

My final question was, "What does democracy mean to you?" She responded, "Everyone has the right to freedom of speech." "No, Ellen, not the first amendment, democracy," I said.

Democracy requires us, as citizens, to stay informed about public issues, to watch carefully how our political leaders and representatives use their powers, and to express our opinions and interests to protect our civic and constitutional rights.

Ellen's response was to retort, "I'm not discussing this any further. Everyone should respect the President!" as she stormed out of the room. No logic, no reason, no truth, and, yet, a stark example of a White Protestant woman who's a supporter of President Trump.

There is a distinct role that White women hold in American democracy. They have the opportunity to do something that many Black women have already done, which is to untangle and re-examine their collective memory. White women can demand new leadership that has the capacity to nurture America so that our nation can finally define itself within its diverse cultures and heritage, giving way to political and socio-economic growth and empathy.

Juxtaposed to this group of White women, an estimated 94 percent of Black women voters supported

Hillary Clinton in the 2016 presidential election. Though Clinton is representative of a White Protestant woman, she's not representative of the 53 percent of those who voted for Trump. There's is a fundamental difference in her belief system. Clinton was nurtured through a religious context of social justice, uplifting the impoverished, and the understanding of self-value as a woman. Clinton believes in democracy not in order to empower men, but rather to empower women, men, and children. During a 2017 interview as part of her What Happened book tour she said:

> *"Women will be under tremendous pressure – and I'm talking principally about White women. They will be under tremendous pressure from fathers and husbands and boyfriends and male employers not to vote for 'the girl'."* [18]

Black women, both married and single, often connect deeply with Clinton. This is in part because Black women tend to see their fate as being connected with that of all women. Unlike Latino and White women, Black women are more likely to be the primary breadwinners in their families, as well as the more educated partner when they marry. Therefore, their politics tend not to lean towards the primary interests of men.

Reverend Dr. Martin Luther King, Jr. said in Strength to Love, "There is a deep understanding for the need of agape; a love that is concerned with going the extra mile to ensure the well-being of others." But this presents challenges. How does one love a person one hates, even while deeming oneself a Christian? How does one deconstruct false memories that dwell in the invisible enterprise of their hearts, that show Black men as rapists or murderers when there's no evidence to support it? How do White women address the misappropriated memories within their race to give way to truth rather than lies, to avoid birthing further racism? Additionally, how does the mother, who gives life, provide for a nation a new moment of nurturing in a world that sees herself as the other?

My mother often tells me, "Though I didn't birth you in my womb, I did birth you in my heart." What's in the heart matters. How do we deconstruct the matters of the heart so that America can yet have another rebirth filled with love and empathy?

In the midst of the litany of memories is there a deeper empire that lurks in these White women's minds, within this invisible empire? Most importantly, how do we unpack the falsehoods that are embedded in their invisible hearts, so truth can surface and lies can be defeated? It is truth bound in love, not lies, that can help heal the soul of America.

CHAPTER FOUR

Strangers Sharing Egypt: Go Down Moses

> *"When Israel was in Egypt's land,*
> *Let my people go;*
> *Oppress'd so hard they could not stand,*
> *Let my people go.*
> *Go down, Moses, way down in Egypt's land.*
> *Tell old Pharaoh –*
> *Let my people go."* [1]

'Go Down Moses' is an American Negro spiritual. It describes events in the Hebrew Cannon, the Torah – the Old Testament of the Christian Bible – specifically Exodus 8:1: "And the LORD spake unto Moses, 'Go unto Pharaoh, and say unto him, Thus saith the LORD, Let my people go, that they may serve me.'"[2] God is commanding Moses to demand the release of the

Israelites from bondage in Egypt. The opening verse is as published by the Jubilee Singers in 1872.

In the song, 'Israel' represents the African American slaves, while 'Egypt' and 'Pharaoh' represent the slave master.[3] Going 'down' to Egypt is derived from the Torah, the Old Testament, recognizing the Nile Valley as lower than Jerusalem and the Promised Land; thus, going to Egypt means going 'down'[4] while going away from Egypt is 'up'. In the context of American slavery, this ancient sense of 'down' converged with the concept of 'down the river' (the Mississippi River), where slaves' conditions were notoriously worse, a situation which gave rise to the idiom 'to sell [someone] down the river', still used in present-day English.[5] It is within the context of this 'sacred text' that the African American experience identifies with that of Israel, the Jewish experience.

In Deborah, Golda, and Me: Being Female and Jewish in America, published in 1991, Letty Cottin Pogrebin asserts that the African American-Jewish relationship rests on a common history of oppression.

> *"Both African-Americans and Jews have known Egypt," she wrote. "Jews have*

known it as certain death (the killing of the
firstborn, then the ovens and gas chambers).
African-Americans have known it as death
and terror by bondage." [6]

It is true that since the time of slavery African Americans have modelled their lives in a variety of ways on the metaphor of the bondage of a Jewish stranger in a foreign land. African Americans have long believed that there was still a vast racial gulf separating the two groups. No matter how much they were both enslaved and treated like strangers, during the decades preceding the birth of the Civil Rights movement many African Americans saw Jews as having the privilege of White skin. The 'great fault line'[7] in America, they felt, was not between the oppressors and the oppressed, including Jews, but between those with White skin and those without.[8]

Another undeniable difference between the two peoples' suffering stood out. In 1967, the author and activist James Baldwin warned liberal Jews that their image of a close Black-Jewish affinity was "a fiction of their imagination", and that candour and realism were now required.[9] "The Jewish travail occurred across the sea and America was a place of rescue for him from the house of bondage," Baldwin wrote. "But America is the house of bondage for the Negro, and no country can rescue him."[10]

Yet, during the twentieth century several eminent figures saw and were moved by the similarities between both the faiths and the histories of Jews and African Americans. Julius Rosenwald, the son of German-Jewish immigrants, rose to become one of the wealthiest men in America. A humanitarian who was much influenced by the social Gospel of Rabbi Emil Hirsch of Chicago Sinai Congregation, Rosenwald used his great wealth and talent for leadership for 'tikkun olam' (healing the world).[11] In total he gave away $63 million to various causes (over $630 million in today's dollars).

Rosenwald led the establishment of social services for 100,000 impoverished Jewish immigrants in Chicago, Illinois. His philanthropy took a dramatic turn after reading works by African American thinkers. The story of the partnership between Julius Rosenwald and Booker T. Washington is a compelling one. Washington, who was the head of the Tuskegee Institute, approached Julius Rosenwald in 1912 to ask him to help fund economic advancement for African

American southerners through vocational education at the college. It was also Rosenwald who spurred the establishment of a total of 25 Young Men's Christian Associations (YMCA) and Young Women's Christian Associations (YWCA) – the first to serve African Americans – in cities across the United States.[12]

In recent history, however, not all followers of America's two largest faith groups have felt that combating racism is a cause they should actively espouse. The great Christian religious leader of the Civil Rights movement of the 1960s, the Reverend Dr. Martin Luther King, Jr., had to repeatedly argue that the Judeo-Christian tradition, properly interpreted, designated racism as a sin and therefore an evil that all religious leaders must address.[13]

Yet, as an American society founded on a hunger and thirst for religious freedom was turning a deaf ear to the pleas of a marginalized people, certain that God's creation suffered no stratification, a few like-minded humanitarians, across racial identities, were leading the charge for equality.

In January 1963, at a conference for Christian and Jewish leaders in Chicago, King met Rabbi Abraham

Joshua Heschel, a Polish-born émigré from New York. The two men shared a common passion for preaching, social justice, and activism, and they quickly formed a true bond. "Martin Luther King is a sign that God has not forsaken the United States of America," said Heschel.[14] In his opening address to the conference Heschel reminded Jews and African Americans of their shared history of slavery and oppression:

> *"Pharaoh is not ready to capitulate. The exodus began, but is far from having been completed. In fact, it was easier for the children of Israel to cross the Red Sea than for a Negro to cross certain university campuses."*

Exhorting his audience to do 'tikkun olam' and fight against the "eye disease" of racism, Heschel concluded with his favourite verse, Amos 5:24: "Let justice roll down like waters, and righteousness like a mighty stream."

King and Heschel went on to work in close partnership in the Civil Rights movement. During the 1965 protest march from Selma to Montgomery they walked together in the front row of marchers; "I felt my legs were praying," his daughter, Susannah Heschel shared that he later wrote in his diary.[15] Heschel's public support for King stirred many members of the Jewish community to take part in the struggle for Civil Rights.

Earlier, in the summer of 1964, the Student Nonviolent Coordinating Committee's Freedom Summer project brought to Mississippi about a thousand mainly White and wealthy northern students, more than a quarter of whom were Jewish. They would join thousands of Black Mississippian volunteers in a heroic effort to register as many African American voters as they could, and to run Freedom Schools and community centres to help local Black communities.[16]

Many of Mississippi's White residents were furious at this sudden influx of young activists attempting to bring about a change in the status quo. From the start, the volunteers were subjected to a relentless campaign of violence and harassment. On their very first day, one Black and two Jewish activists were abducted and killed by members of the Klu Klux Klan. Their bodies were not found until six weeks later. Over the course of Freedom Summer, volunteers were subjected to arrests, beatings, and drive-by shootings, while homes, businesses, churches, and schools were bombed.

However, despite the fear in which the activists lived – or perhaps in part because of it – many later said that whatever their racial and religious identities, they felt united by a strong sense of community. This was deepened by the singing of songs based on traditional African American spirituals about the struggle for freedom and redemption. Singing these songs also helped marchers to calmly hold their resolve when faced with violent, angry mobs or hostile policemen with dogs. One of the so-called 'Freedom Songs' was the Civil Rights anthem 'Ain't gonna let nobody turn me 'round':

> *"Ain't gonna let nobody, Turn me 'round,*
>
> *Ain't gonna let nobody, Turn me 'round, Turn me 'round.*
>
> *I'm gonna keep on walkin', Keep on talkin', Marchin' into freedom land!"* [17]

America is still grappling with religious justifications of racial discrimination designed to relegate 'the stranger' to the margins of society. Being the stranger in America is no longer the sole experience of African Americans and Jews – since the mass migration of Hispanics and Latinos it now impacts them too. The stranger is the other.

Even more daunting are the children who are in Pharaoh's concentration camp in cages at the border with Mexico. In 2018, U.S. Attorney General Jeff Sessions and President Donald Trump dehumanized migrant children and labelled them as criminals. Sessions defended this action by citing passages of Holy Scripture once used by segregationists to perpetuate slavery, segregation, White nationalism, and Jim Crow. Dr. Barbara Reynolds said to me, "The 'make America great again' rhetoric appears to be inciting the Attorney General and his cronies to thump the Bible, while self-righteously and piously practising a new breed of spirituality that encompasses 'hate thy neighbour'."

Sessions clearly misses the fundamental message of the Scripture, which Jesus quoted as Good News, not the lies, harsh words, and meanness we see today. Jesus, declaring his mission in Luke 4:18, said that he was anointed "to preach the Gospel (good news) to the poor, heal the broken-hearted, and preach deliverances to the captives to set at liberty them that are bruised." The Attorney General is even at odds with the official declarations of his own United Methodist Church, which in 2016 said:

> *"The fear and anguish so many migrants in the United States live under are due to federal raids, indefinite detention, and deportations which tear apart families and create an atmosphere of panic. Millions of immigrants are denied legal entry to the U.S. due to quotas and race and class barriers, even as employers seek their labor. With the legal avenues closed, immigrants who come in order to support their families must live in the shadows and in intense exploitation and fear. In the face of these unjust laws and the systematic deportation of migrants instituted by the Department of Homeland Security, God's people must stand in solidarity with the migrants in our midst."* [18]

Whereas it can be argued that sacred text is subjective, it can have proper exegeses rather than hateful eisegesis. The use of a Biblical passage to justify punishing immigrants – most of whom are Brown or Black, and came from what President Trump has labelled "shithole countries" – is simply wrong and egregious. These programmes are designed by the Pharisees of today. They turn to Scripture to find passages to support their harmful anti-Black, anti-women, anti-poor policies, which are so void of love and kindness they have no relevance in our modern world. The Trump administration's policies towards the stranger have nothing to do with the Good News, Jesus, the Bible, or anything sacred that is a part of the Jewish, Christian, or Islamic faiths.

Paul, who wrote around 60 A.D., was an apostle of love reflecting the virtues of Jesus Christ. He wrote: "If there be any other commandment, it is summed up in this word, namely, love thy neighbour as thy self. Love works no ill to his neighbour; love therefore is the fulfilment of the law." In Romans 13, Paul writes that Christians are both citizens of the state and the Church, and have a duty to obey both. Very boldly, however, Paul clearly writes in that same passage that love is the foundation of the Gospel, which supersedes all other man-made laws.

Jesus's social Gospel would awaken the Pharisees of his day, namely the lawyers and members of legalistic communities. Having a heart for the injustices of humanity, Jesus condemned that group as "hypocrites" for "straining at gnats and swallowing camels" and omitting the more important areas of the law, which are "judgement, mercy, and faith". He condemned the "sin" of legalism.

Legalists can quote, pound, and thump the Bible, while being ignorant of or oblivious to the spirit of the Law, which exhorts the soul and conscience to be kind, merciful, and charitable. How can they see the sin in abortion but not in the Environmental Protection Agency's policies that allow corporations to leak harmful chemicals into poor neighbourhoods? Or in the Trump administration using the budget to deny healthcare to the medically indigent? Or in encouraging corporate greed? Or in diverting funds allotted to defence to build a wall to keep out 'the stranger'? These kinds of tactics, no doubt, are why Jesus declared: "It is easier for a camel to go through the eye of a needle than for a rich person to enter the kingdom of God."[19]

So why are so many preachers, pastors, bishops, and megachurch leaders not pushing back, defending the sacred text, and taking these Pharisees to task, not only for their punitive practices towards immigrants, but also for the transference of billions of dollars from the needy?

Isn't sacred text worth defending? For how long will loving and moral Americans tolerate hypocrisy, cruelty, and sins against humanity? Is it time for those like Sessions to have a road-to-Damascus experience so that they can get knocked off their high horses and see the light of Jesus's love for the least of these?

The role of faith today

It was Black preachers of the Civil Rights movement who led the singing of freedom songs. It was their exegesis of the Apostle Paul's letter to the Church at Ephesus that underlined that we should not just wrestle against flesh and blood, but against principalities, against powers, against the rulers of the darkness of this world, against spiritual wickedness in high places. They understood that the rulers had to change, but also that there was a need for individuals of all races, religions, and identities to join with them to discuss their similar cultural, political, and social views and to protest. Their collective commitment towards wanting civility brought about the introduction of Acts intended to enshrine in law equality of opportunity for all people, regardless of their colour, gender, religion, or sexuality. They hoped this movement would not just be for America but would become global. And that is what it became.

As we face what feels like either a rebirth or an awakening of ethnic and racial ills, I believe now is the time for us to coalesce, with common faith – to 'tikkun olam', to make the world a better place.

Reverend Dr. Martin Luther King, Jr. when he wrote Strength to Love said that there is a deep understanding for the need of agape, a love that is concerned with going the extra mile to ensure the well-being of others.[20]

King believed in a better world, but in order to attain his vision he argued that we must first face our fears and then master these fears through courage, love, and faith. He preached of the courage that all should show in their non-violent stand against segregation, and he believed that all people could possess this courage because we are all made in the image of God. This courage is the strength to hope for better days, the strength to have faith in our Lord, and most of all, the strength to love all of God's children no matter their skin colour, no matter what their difference.

Within the core of every faith is love:

- **Judaism** – teaches to "Love the stranger as thyself."[21]

- **Islam** – teaches that "None of you has faith until he loves for his brother what he loves for himself."[22]

- **Christianity** – teaches that God himself gave up the life of a beloved son for the sake of love.[23]

And, in so many other beliefs and traditions there's this same key element of love. You may ask how we are going to achieve equality, justice, righteousness, and being 'right' one with another? I would answer that we will only do so when we persist without failing to have the 'strength to love'.

CHAPTER FIVE

Bitter Sweet: From Slavery to Freedom and Beyond the Colour Line

"Well I don't have no mother, father, brother, sister,
boy, I ain't never seen
Well you know sometime I feel so lonesome
Well yes I feel just like I wanna scream ...
... Oh Lord, boy I gotta take the bitter with the sweet."[1]

On May 25, 2020 in Minneapolis, Minnesota, a 46-year-old Black man called George Floyd was arrested after a convenience store employee called the police because Floyd had purchased cigarettes with a counterfeit $20 bill. Seventeen minutes after the first squad car arrived at the scene, Floyd was unconscious and pinned beneath three police officers, showing no signs of life.

By combining videos from bystanders and security cameras, it was revealed that the officers' actions violated the policies of the Minneapolis Police Department and Floyd's civil and human rights. As he suffocated, Floyd cried out, "I can't breathe!", and even called for his dead "Mama" while onlookers begged the officers to get off him.[2]

This tragic murder has awakened a new level of public awareness of both systemic and institutional racism. Racism is the overt, longstanding devaluing of those whose skin is rich in the pigment melanin. A natural sunscreen, high levels of melanin make a people's skin darker while protecting it from the many harmful effects of ultraviolet rays.[3] Yet no amount of melanin can protect those who have shades of brown skin from the vile hatred of some of those who do not. Melanin cannot protect those with shades of brown skin from being demeaned, marginalized, and occasionally even murdered by others, simply because of the colour of their outer layer.

The current-day Civil Rights movement Black Lives Matter[4] (BLM) is engaged in a global attempt to end the brutal killing of those who have shades of brown skin by those who have power. BLM's origins and efforts are rooted in the truths of the transatlantic slave trade.

Slavery is a painful and difficult part of the world's history. Visits to the Smithsonian National Museum of African American History and Culture, in Washington, D.C., begin below ground with an exhibit called 'Slavery and Freedom'. It displays a piece of the hull of a Portuguese slave ship that sank off the coast of South Africa in 1794, taking 212 of the 500 slaves shackled on board to their deaths.[5] They were on their way to toil to boost the wealth of a distant imperial power by producing 'white gold', better known as sugar. Chosen simply because of the melanin in their skin, the African slaves' back-breaking efforts on plantations caused them to become a prime commodity themselves. They were vital cogs in a vast international machine that generated previously unimagined riches for a tiny, powerful elite. The sweetness of one group of people's successes created the bitterness of another people's long struggle for freedom.

The racist brutality we are seeing today is not merely being made visible because of the availability of recording devices on modern smart phones. Such acts have their parallels in centuries of the devaluing, dehumanizing, and desecrating of Black bodies. The long history of the transatlantic slave trade looms over us all – some are conscious of it, some are not. Yet we are all aware of the differences between people that exist in this world – and that the skin that protects us from the sun's ultraviolet rays does not make us invulnerable.

An upheaval is now underway – from the United Kingdom to the United States and beyond, representations of slave traders are being hoisted from their prominent positions. The decapitation of a statue of Christopher Columbus in Boston, Massachusetts,[6] along with the removal of Robert Milligan's statue from outside the Museum of London[7] are attempts by some to erase bitter-sweet histories.

The Italian explorer Christopher Columbus is celebrated as having 'discovered' the New World. The colonization of the Americas and the exploitation of its native peoples would swiftly follow, as would the opening up of the transatlantic trade routes that would ultimately deliver African slaves to the New World colonies to produce sugar. By the time of his death, the Scot Robert Milligan owned two sugar plantations and 526 slaves in Jamaica. This history can't simply be dissolved by taking down bronze and stone figures.

History is our opportunity to place an inquiry upon the past. It is an investigative study of what happened. It's an umbrella of past events that is filled with memories, discoveries, collections, objects, and artefacts. History encompasses the many ways in which past events are organized, presented, and interpreted.

History serves to narrate, describe, examine, question, and analyze a sequence of those past events. Its role is to probe and scrutinize the patterns of cause and effect. It is the place where we debate, interrogate, correct, and even expand our knowledge. It is a place of new revelations surrounding what once happened – it is a place of exploring culture[8] and heritage, even that of legends and myths, the real and surreal. What history is not is something that should be erased, like pulling the pages out of a book or wiping the words off a white board. No, that's not what you do with history.

But rather you take it to build upon. History should be broadened and balanced, so that it can expose, heal, and redeem, for truth-telling. It should equip us with more – more facts, more depth, more understanding, and more revelation.

We have entered into a new era of wide-ranging public debate about the fate of public historical symbols: buildings, statues, street names. These long-awaited conversations about divided history in local and national communities should be viewed as places for constructive discussions to explore practical resolutions. This is where we can create brave spaces to shape narratives that inform the past and frame the future.

All public symbols represent different and ever-changing meanings and values for the people who view them, in relation to their own knowledge and understanding of the past, the present, and their hopes for the future. This is not a time to destroy contested objects that represent injustice or hatred. But rather it is an opportunity for communities to explore 'what happened' – to address despair, anger, and frustration, along with meanings and values that remain unrecognized and misunderstood. It is vital to comprehend the bitter-sweet history of a people – that of melanin-rich people's human bodies – and why they often appear to be less valued than are mere material symbols.

In May 1892, in Memphis, Tennessee, Edward Carmack, a White supremacist newspaper publisher and politician, incited a mob to destroy the newspaper office of pioneering Black journalist Ida B. Wells. This incident led to Ida B. Wells' 1894 four-month speaking tour in England, where she sought to solicit international pressure on the United States government to stop the lynching of Black people. Wells also encouraged the boycott of American cotton (not sugar, because in the U.S. tobacco and cotton were now generating the nation's wealth).

Wells wrote, "The appeal to the white man's pocket has ever been more effectual than all the appeals ever made to his conscience." She understood that economic pressure was the only thing that would gain the attention of those who profited from oppressing others.[9]

Wells went to England because that nation had long grappled with slavery. She knew of the great English abolitionists who had stood up against the brutality of slavery. Wells' fellow Methodist William Wilberforce, a statesman and radical reformist, had played a crucial part in bringing about the abolition of slavery in most of the British Empire.

It was Wilberforce who rose in the House of Commons in London on May 12, 1789, and said: "When I consider the magnitude of the subject which I am to bring before the House – a subject in which the interests, not of this country, nor of Europe alone, but of the whole world, and of posterity, are involved: and when I think, at the same time, on the weakness of the advocate who has undertaken this great cause – when these reflections press upon my mind, it is impossible for me not to feel both terrified and concerned at my own inadequacy to such a task."[10]

He went on to talk about his reflection through the course of a long and laborious process of self-questioning and reasoning. He described how the strength of his conviction had grown within his own mind and soul. Four years earlier, Wilberforce had read The Rise and Progress of Religion in the Soul[11] by the English nonconformist leader, educator, and hymn-writer, Philip Doddridge. In Doddridge's book the human heart is examined as the source of a person's faith, goodness, and meaning.

Wilberforce ended his slavery abolitionist speech with these words: "When I turn myself to these thoughts, I take courage – I determine to forget all my other fears, and I march forward with a firmer step in the full assurance that my cause will bear me out, and that I shall be able to justify upon the clearest principles every resolution in my hand, the avowed end of which is the total abolition of the slave trade."[12]

This impassioned cry is known to have a played a key role in the abolition of the slave trade in the British Empire in 1807.[13] However, it was not until 1833 – the year when Wilberforce transitioned from the earth – that the Slavery Abolition Act abolished slavery itself.[14] In the U.S., the terrible practice would survive for even longer; following the Union's victory in the Civil War, slavery was outlawed by the ratification of the 13th Amendment in 1865.[15]

Britain has a complicated relationship with its historical links to slavery. Although it was, in fact, slaves themselves who started the fight against slavery, the British authorities have long had a tendency to claim the credit for abolition, while shying away from highlighting the key role that the nation played in the transatlantic slave trade. There is little public awareness, even today, of the vast sums the British government paid in compensation to the owners of slaves freed in the Caribbean colonies after abolition

– about £16 billion in today's money. The debt was so huge, British taxpayers were paying to line the pockets of slave owners' descendants until 2015.[16]

However, Ida B. Wells did find solace in the English anti-slavery campaigners, people who were deeply driven by their faith. Those who understood the value of the other and used their feet and faith, their voices and power, to dismantle this bitter-sweet moment that has forever stained world history.

In the summer of 2020, a statute of the same Edward Carmack who set fire to Ida B. Well's office, was destroyed in Memphis.[17] For the iconoclasts, the eradication of a symbol of oppression and violation was gratifying. However, the removal of a statue does not erase the history. It simply erases the symbol.

The history of a multi-century institution of brutality and exploitation remains. The legacy of decades of state-sanctioned racial apartheid and inequality, in every area of life, remains omnipresent. Imagine how much discussion could occur if a statue of Ida B. Wells was erected just opposite a statue of Carmack so that they could face each other into eternity. They both existed. They are both part of this complicated reality.

If, as societies, we engage in deep and meaningful discussion and interpretation, then no history will need to be erased – the bitter or the sweet. We can be honest about how racists sowed the seeds of hatred and destruction across entire continents. And we can teach our fellow citizens about the brave individuals who fought for freedom and equality.

We can allow healing to begin if we create opportunities to set out the broad historical context around what we call race, and interpret past events more thoughtfully. This could be achieved, for example, if close to every contested statue, building, or street-name sign, education programmes in institutions and municipalities were willing to add panels or markers telling the entire story. Such moves would also enable us to better preserve, curate, and confront our often difficult and complex histories.

If we take up the challenge now of recounting those difficult histories in ways that explore past conflicts openly and represent all of our true selves, perhaps 200 years from now we will see progress. Rather than throwing history into the harbour to erode – as though none of it ever happened – we can use it to build a better world for all.

So, how do we move beyond this dreadful stain on world history, the horror that still looms with the devaluing of Brown bodies? We embrace otherness. We create brave spaces. And we combine them, in order to learn not just about ourselves, but about who is the other. We need to have the courage to discuss our mutual fears and concerns, our fragility and power, our difference and our alikeness.

I believe that we must gather ourselves, with common purpose and cause, to analyse race, culture, systemic privileges, and other social phenomena that have generated damaging perceptions and group behaviours in relation to the soul. Then we must build on this knowledge to embrace our collective humanity – so that no one is deemed sub-human, and without a soul or meaning.

I believe it's time to move beyond the pervasive false construct of race. I also think it will take generations to fully achieve this. I understand the urgency of now, but we shouldn't fool ourselves that we can dismantle systemic racism – which has been embedded in societal norms for centuries – merely by protesting or by toppling statues. White people should not tell themselves that it will be enough to occasionally hear about Black history, nor should they believe that having a Black friend or family member makes them different. There is real work to be done. And to undertake it, we will all have to fully engage our ethereal essence, the core of our mutual morality. We will all have to become tuned-in to our souls.

Perhaps I'm strange, but I seem to have an internal compass that is forever set towards hope. Is it truly hard to believe that this bitter-sweet journey from slavery to freedom will one day lead us beyond the colour line – on the condition that we, as a global society, commit to the hard work that lies ahead?

CHAPTER SIX

Fathers of a Nation: Black Men Vote Too

"R – E – S – P –E – C – T

Find out what it means to me

R – E – S – P –E – C – T

Take care, TCB"[1]

The battle to 'Restore America's Soul' was Joe Biden's presidential campaign slogan. After an overly congested democratic primary, Biden became the 2020 presumptive nominee. It appears that, for Biden, soul is neither a homage to his Roman Catholic upbringing nor a nod to having enjoyed a Chicago Southside Sunday dinner prepared by Marian Robinson (Michelle Obama's mother). Instead, Biden asserts that his presidency will create policies that reflect our shared values. It is also a commitment to return integrity to the office of the President of the United States. While some, and a majority of people colour, feel President Donald Trump has sullied the office, there are others, most of whom are White, who feel former President Barack Obama created an environment in which they needed to try to 'take the country back'.

Over a decade ago, the leadership of the GOP erupted in fear over Obama ascending to the presidency. There seemed to be concern that a Soul Fest would break out at the White House. The South Lawn would host picnics with fried chicken and watermelon. The helipad would be transformed into a dance floor for Electric Slide and a Soul Train line. The Queen of Soul[2] would hold an impromptu concert from the Truman Balcony belting out 'R-E-S-P-E-C-T!' Oh, and maybe over in the Rose Garden there'd even be a scramble board revealing the week's notable African American history, and, of course, over in the Jackie Kennedy Garden, several card tables for spades and dominoes.

For eight years, love it or hate it, the country got to experience the souls of President Barack Obama and his family. June 2020 made five years since President Trump had announced his candidacy, and during that time the country and the world have gotten to know his soul.

The meaning of the term 'soul' varies depending on a number of dynamics. Some psychologists have identified the soul as the immaterial essence and totality of who you are at a core level – your true nature. Mateo Sol suggests that the soul either gravitates towards light or darkness, depending on how one's ego is developed. An ego is usually constructed from a collection of memories and beliefs about who you are, where you came from, and how you define the meaning of 'good' and 'bad'.[3]

President Trump's ego led him to create his mantra of 'Make America Great Again'[4] – arguably, a call for America's restoration. Trump emerged to champion the hatred and racism that ensued after Mitch McConnell's failed attempt to make Obama a one-term president. The blatant disrespect of Congressman Joe Wilson's shouting of "You lie!"[5] during Obama's 2009 joint session of Congress was also seeded with core values: those that were brewing within some members of the Republican party.

This group had disdain for a Black man who had sworn to uphold America's most revered document, the U.S. Constitution.[6] When the Constitution was written in 1787, the Founding Fathers did not deem the Negro slave to be a citizen, or even a person. It wouldn't be until 1867, following the Civil War, that slavery would be abolished everywhere in America. A Republican-dominated Congress passed the First Reconstruction Act,[7] which divided the South into military districts and outlined a new government based on male suffrage. This opened the way for the 15th Amendment[8] of 1870, guaranteeing the right of Black men to vote. White men running the Republican party understood the power dynamic of Black men helping them to regain the south.

The day after the 15th Amendment was ratified, Thomas Mundy Peterson[9] of Perth Amboy, New Jersey, became the first Black man to vote. By the late 1870s, more than 20 Black men served in Congress, with more than 600 serving in state legislatures and many more in local offices. The same Republican party, however, effectively nullified both the 14th Amendment[10] (which guaranteed citizenship with all privileges to Black men) and the 15th Amendment

– stripping African Americans in the south of their right to vote.

The ensuing decades bore witness to various discriminatory and voter-suppression practices: poll taxes and literacy tests, along with Jim Crow laws,[11] intimidation, and outright violence were used to prevent Blacks from exercising their right to vote. It was not until 1965 that the Voting Rights Act would prohibit racial discrimination in voting. The act was the result of campaigning led by Black men, including Reverend Dr. Martin Luther King, Jr., Reverend Ralph Abernathy, and Andrew Young, who went on to serve in Congress, as U.N. Ambassador, and as Mayor of Atlanta. There were also Black women aligned with them in the fight for voting, freedom, and equality.

An estimated 30 million Black Americans are eligible to vote in 2020, according to the Pew Research Center.[12] While Black women are rightfully celebrated as anchors of the Democratic Party, Black men also have a long history of voting Democrat. According to a 2019 report by the Center for American Progress States of Change,[13] 78 percent of Black men with a college degree voted for Hillary Clinton in 2016 (16 percent voted for Trump) and 82 percent of Black men without a college degree voted Democrat (11 percent voted for Trump).

In August 2015, I was in Cleveland, Ohio, attending the memorial services of a mentor and fraternity brother, Congressman Louis Stokes. After the services, I took an Uber to go to a dinner with members of the Congressional Black Caucus. The driver was a married 54-year-old Black male, father of three, and native of Cleveland. And he was a Trump supporter. He had lost his construction job during Obama's administration. He felt that because Trump had built hotels all over the world, as president he would put Black men back to work. And, of course, Trump had a reputation, as the celebrity boss from The Apprentice, for having given chances to ordinary people. I sat in that car for 90 minutes (for which I paid a $100 bill instead of the original $12), missing the dinner. When I finally got out of the car, shaking my head in disbelief, I said to myself, "If conversations like that are happening in barbershops, Donald Trump is going to win."

During the 2018 midterm election, according to the U.S. Census Bureau, 49 percent of Americans voted. There was only a two percentage-point differential in comparison with non-Hispanic Blacks, who voted at a rate of 47 percent.[14] Though Black men are committed to voting, they are more focused on survival – and making it happen for themselves. There's a long-held struggle with their roles in politics. So, the first rule of nature, self-preservation for the day, overrides all else. For some, the immediate results of neither Obama nor Trump has delivered a crumb, let alone a slice of the American pie.

Whereas criminal-justice reform, free and subsidized childcare, keeping the family safe and, sure, marijuana legalization are important to Black men, the basics of sustainability and wealth creation have been missing under both recent administrations. More than anything, Black men want equality and an opportunity to fully live the American Dream of providing for their families and amassing wealth. They don't want to build skyline condominiums they can't own. Nor do they want to pave roads upon which they can't drive the same cars. Most importantly, Black men know that they are directly descended from the 'commodity' that built America's wealth – the free slave labour of the sugar industry. Today, many Black men are still the 'products' of privatized prisons. Black men are no longer interested in being counted as inmates or voters, but instead want to be fully included as citizens in a nation in which the government and society are accountable to their needs.

In W.E.B. Du Bois' seminal collection of essays, The Souls of Black Folks, written in 1903, he pens 'Of the Sons of Master and Man'.[15] In it, Du Bois discusses physical proximity, economic strategy, and politics – the power of the ballot in every state. He reveals the police system as having been designed to control slaves and explains how courts can be the means of re-enslaving Blacks. Crucially, he addresses the issue of the lack of social contact, stating: "There is almost no community of intellectual life or point of transference where the thoughts and feelings of one race can come into direct contact and sympathy with thoughts and feelings of the other." He concludes: "The future of the South depends on the ability of the representatives of these opposing views to see and appreciate and sympathize with each other's position."[16] Du Bois was speaking to the soul of a nation. He was not completely heard then, but we should really listen and take action now to restore or even discover the true soul of America.

For Biden's clarion 'soul' call to resonate with Black men, with his election as 46th President of the United States, it must be about accountability, rather than the political rhetoric and empty promises portrayed by many public officials. Also, Biden must give a more honest account of his involvement in the Violent Crime Control and Law Enforcement Act,[17] now known as the 1994 Crime Law.

On May 14, 2019, during one of his campaign events, Biden, was questioned about the bill's intended punishments. His response was: "Let's get something straight: 92 out of every 100 prisoners who end up behind bars are in a state prison, not a federal prison. This idea that the crime bill generated mass incarceration – it did not generate mass incarceration."[18] Nah, Joe, you've got to do better than that. According to the Sentencing Project's June 2019 paper 'Felony Disenfranchisement: A Primer',[19] currently one out of 13 Blacks can't vote due to a felony connection. Want to guess how many are Black men? Where's the federal bill to rightfully protect and restore their voting rights?

The Crime Law also separated fathers (and mothers) from children, community, and work. And, yes, it was the catalyst for harsh sentencing guidelines that placed

Black men behind bars in states that disenfranchised them. T-Bone got locked up over a dime bag and Ray-Ray for transporting firearms. However, both industries are being run by 'the man' not Black men. These are both examples of men, however misguided, trying to catch a piece of the American Dream. Instead they got from 20 years to life in prison, taking away their promise and some of the hopes of their children.

The Bible, in Genesis 2:7, says: "God formed man of the dust of the ground and breathed into his nostrils the breath of life, and man became a living soul." That soul became the father of nations. Despite Biden's stance on the 1994 Crime Law, a Biden vote, for the Biden win, now has the potential to breathe life into Black men. Biden has spoken to the reason for his stance and has undergirded his candidacy and forthcoming administration with Black men to envision an America of promise together. This reality will afford the much-awaited chance for them to become vital leaders and fathers of and within the nation.

It is time for America to create scales of economic, political, and social justice that lean towards uplifting all Black men, instead of tolerating structural racism that works to their detriment. No longer are Black men satisfied being mere fishermen; it's time to own oceans. No longer is it enough for them to form the vast majority of the NFL's athletic talent; it's time for ownership. Black men want to feel the lifeblood flowing through their veins and arteries. They want to create fulfilling lives, which woven together with opportunity and promise, comprise a nation with rhythm and balance.

How does the world begin to see Black men as the fathers of a nation, rather than as commodities, beasts, and unhuman? Barack Obama didn't resolve this issue by being elected president. Nor did President Trump cause America to re-examine it, but rather increased the divisions in society. The missing element is simple and yet vitally important:

R – E – S – P –E – C – T.

CHAPTER SEVEN

The Soul of a Nation: Courage for the Constitution

"Hey, do you know about the U.S.A.? Do you know about the government? Can you tell me about the Constitution? Hey, learn about the U.S.A.

In 1787, I'm told Our Founding Fathers did agree to write a list of principles For keepin' people free." [1]

As a child growing up in the bayou of Louisiana, life was filled with splendour and culture. For me, as a southern hue of Brown American (commonly referenced as Black), my world was filled with 'soul'. Soul in my world consisted of two things – food and music. I spent Saturday mornings captivated by two TV shows, both with music at their core. The first was Soul Train,[2] the theme song of which was:

> "People all over the world
>
> People all over the world
>
> It's time, it's time to get down."[3]

There were two enduring elements of Soul Train. The scramble board, where two dancers were given 60 seconds to unscramble a set of letters that spelled the name of that show's performer or a notable person in African American history. And of course, the Soul Train line, in which some of the dancers formed two lines with a space in the middle for the rest of the dancers to strut and boogie down.

The other show I loved was a bit more educational, but it also was set to music – Schoolhouse Rock![4] I would sing my heart out to 'Conjunction-Junction, what's your function?' and 'Lolly, Lolly, Lolly, get your adverbs here'. But the one that had the most meaning was 'The Preamble':

> "Hey, do you know about the U.S.A.?
>
> Do you know about the government?
>
> Can you tell me about the Constitution?
>
> Hey, learn about the U.S.A."[5]

It goes on tell you about how in 1787 the Founding Fathers sat down and wrote a list of rules and called it the U.S. Constitution. The first part of the Constitution is called 'The Preamble' and it explains what those Founding Fathers set out to do. And I would sing along at the top of my lungs:

"We the people, in order to form a more perfect Union

Establish justice, insure domestic tranquillity

Provide for the common defence

Promote the general welfare, and

Secure the blessings of liberty

To ourselves and our posterity

Do ordain and establish this Constitution for the United States of America."

My world consisted of soul and of being American. Little did I know in my childhood reality that this U.S. Constitution was not drawn up with people of my heritage in mind. Throughout this revered document's articles, crafted to free the young nation from Great Britain, was the language of 'person and citizen'. And yet these terms were specific to those whom the Founding Fathers deemed to be both people and citizens – in other words, White men. The Negro and women, namely White women, were excluded.

The journey towards full suffrage would be a painfully slow and winding one for these excluded groups, but the fight often saw them unite in a common cause. The American social reformer and abolitionist Frederick Douglass[6] and the social reformer and women's rights activist Susan B. Anthony[7] met in 1848 and became close friends and allies, campaigning together for both abolition and women's suffrage. After the Civil War, however, the relationship was strained when Frederick Douglass adopted a gradualist position and wanted to concentrate on rights for African Americans first. Douglass feared that trying to achieve universal suffrage all at once would be too difficult. Anthony, who was worried that progressing in steps would inevitably stop short of full universal suffrage, viewed Douglass's stance as a betrayal.

In 1867, when the U.S. Constitution was eighty years old, the Republican-dominated Congress passed the First Reconstruction Act following the Union victory in the Civil War and the subsequent abolition of slavery. The act outlined how the new southern states' governments were to be established, specifying that all their male citizens over the age of 21 "of whatever race, color, or previous condition"[8] would be entitled to vote. In 1870 the 15th Amendment was adopted into the U.S. Constitution, giving all Black men across the Union the right to vote. African Americans promptly joined with White allies to elect the Republican Party to power in most of the southern states. Those very states, however, soon set about introducing measures designed to prevent African Americans from exercising their right to vote, leading to many decades of struggle.

For American women, the fight for suffrage would last well into the twentieth century. One of the many brave female campaigners whose efforts paved the way to victory was the former slave Isabelle Baumfree,[9] who upon her conversion to Methodism changed her name to Sojourner Truth. At the 1851 Women's Rights Convention held in Akron, Ohio, she preached one of the most famous abolitionist and women's rights messages in American history, 'Ain't I a Woman?' [10]Truth addressed the issues of the "negroes of the South and the White women at the North", declaring that, "White men will be in a fix pretty soon."

Reverend Truth's concern was that the rights of the Negro woman should not be forgotten. Unlike White women, she said, Black women had never been helped into a carriage or lifted over muddy puddles, but carried their own burden of suffering. Addressing Black men, she said they needed to recognize that, like them, many Black women had endured brutal beatings, as well as seeing their children sold into slavery and "crying a mother's grief". Then Truth turned her attention to faith:

> "Then that little man in black there, he says women can't have as much rights as men, 'cause Christ wasn't a woman! Where did your Christ come from? Where did your Christ come from? From God and a woman! Man had nothing to do with Him. If the first woman God ever made was strong enough to turn the world upside down all alone, these women together ought to be able to turn it back, and get it right side up again!" [11]

The campaigning efforts of Sojourner Truth and Susan B. Anthony, as well as Elizabeth Stanton, Lucretia Mott, and many others, reached fruition on

August 18, 1920, when the 19th Amendment was ratified, granting all women the right to vote.

In the early 1900s, while the southern states were using discrimination, Jim Crow laws, and violence to deny African Americans their civil rights, W.E.B. Du Bois, through his prophetic writings, offered two key theories about the dynamics of race and the future of the Negro.

In his essay 'The Talented 10th',[12] Du Bois described the likelihood that one in ten Black men would become leaders, through methods such as continuing their education, writing books, or becoming directly involved in social change. He argued that 10 percent would give access to the remaining 90 percent and offer a sense of some stabilization for the race.

In 1903 Du Bois published The Souls of Black Folk, in which he outlined his theory that the twentieth century would be dominated by "the problem of the color line"[13] – the relation of the darker to the lighter races of men in Asia and Africa, in the Americas, and the islands of the sea. He addressed the concern that the population of over half the world would be denied the right to obtain and share in the opportunities and privileges of modern civilization, all because of the colour line.

However, nestled in there was Du Bois' use of the term 'double consciousness', perhaps taken from Ralph Waldo Emerson (The Transcendentalist and Fate). 'Double consciousness' described the notion that Black people must have two fields of vision at all times.[14] As well as being conscious of how the world views them, they must be conscious of how they view themselves.

What we all truly thirst for, whatever our gender or the colour of our skin, is justice. The symbol of justice is a lady with weighing scales in her hands. Originally known as the goddess Themis (in Greek Themis means 'order'), her importance today to our laws and legal systems is derived in essence from her stories and ideals.[15] She first appeared in Greek mythology around 800 B.C. as one of the Titan gods. Each god held the power of law, and Themis was the goddess of 'the order of the natural world', organizing things like the seasons, for example. She also ordered the path of a person's life, including the timing of their birth and death. Themis was known to bring balance to justice, and that justice would ultimately thrive within democracy.

The Reverend Dr. Martin Luther King, Jr. preached about the deep understanding for the need of agape; a love that is concerned with going the extra mile to ensure the well-being of others. He believed that we must face our fears and then master these fears through courage, love, and faith in order to achieve a better world.[16]

America needs to remember to have courage. This courage is the strength to hope for better days, the strength to have faith, and most of all, the strength to love all of God's children no matter their skin colour, heritage, language, sexuality, or religion – no matter the difference.

At this time of division, discord, and unrest, America needs healing for its soul. And we are the ones to do it. We need to stand together as a people of common struggles; even if we have polar-opposite beliefs on some issues, we are all united by our humanity. We need to look towards a future that can be all about change – not just for tomorrow, but forever. We must ensure that for the generations to come there will be a U.S. Constitution that protects everyone's citizenship in a society that adheres unwaveringly to its democratic principles. But that takes courage.

We have some hard days ahead, but we can do this. I believe that it is critical, at this moment in history, that those of us who understand the soul and the Constitution of our nation do our duty and fulfil our obligation to protect them both.

In his Republic, Plato poses this question: is it always better to be just than unjust?[17] Socrates suggests an answer – he describes what a good city would be like, saying that a good city would be just. If we define justice as a virtue of a city, Socrates says, that will help us to define it as a virtue of a living person.

"People All Over the World

People All Over the World

It's Time to Get Down

– to the hard work of bring us to the core of justice."

Perhaps there needs to be an echo in our souls of the famous words of the prophetic voice of Don Cornelius, presenter of Soul Train: "And, always, in departing we wish you love, peace, and soul"?[18]

REFLECTIONS

Four of the five articles written by me and included here originally appeared in other publications; where this is the case, the name of the relevant publication and the date are given. In some cases, I have revised parts of those articles for this book.

REFLECTION I

Why Did Jesus Weep: Because #BlackLivesMatter Too?

The Afro-American

September 26, 2016

For the last four visible years America has endured, once again, the polarizing effects of racism and injustice. Yet, instead of the perpetrators wearing white sheets and lynching African Americans with coral ropes as they did earlier decades, they now wear blue uniforms and use issued firearms. The loss of Trayvon, Eric, Tamir, Sandra, Freddie, Korryn, Alton, Terence, Keith, and all of the others we name, came not because their assassins feared them, but because they believed these lives didn't matter. Secretly, I've wept at my core on hearing the news that they have taken yet another life. Whenever I'm driving my car, with my two-year-old, Zayden, I pray that our lives will matter.

As African American lives continue to be disproportionately taken, many onlookers (primarily Millennials), have begun to question ever-more loudly whether those in power believe that #BlackLivesMatter. And if so, why is injustice prevailing in the loss of these lives? The Black Lives Matter movement does not assert that others' lives do not matter. It aims to draw attention to the need for understanding whether those who enact, execute, frame, and inform the law also value Black lives.

In my youth, every evening we had to offer a Scripture, after prayer, before we could partake of supper. We would all eagerly go for "Jesus Wept" because it was the easiest to remember. As I sit most evenings unable to eat, sickened to my stomach, praying, and searching the Scripture for meaning, I ponder why did Jesus weep.

The Scriptures have three accounts of Jesus weeping. The most notable is because he loved Lazarus, and Martha, and Mary. Even knowing that Lazarus would be raised again, Jesus's human nature mourned, because of others' pain and even because of their lack of belief (John 11:5). Jesus also wept when the chosen people failed to keep Jerusalem 'holy' and set apart from other world powers: "He saw the city and wept over it" (Luke 19:41–44). The other prominent account of his weeping is found in a garden (Luke 22:44). Jesus wept sweat "… like great drops of blood", as he prayed to his Father, knowing his time had come to die for a humanity that might never get it.

Why did Jesus weep? Was it because he was fully human and, yet, fully divine, feeling the spiritual and human pain of the people? Was it from his humanity and divinity, that he felt love, disappointment, loss, grief, and sadness – every human emotion that evokes tears from the heart?

One doesn't have to be dead to grieve over death and dying. Grieving calls us into an experience of raw immediacy that is often devastating. In A Grief Observed, a collection of reflections on the experience of bereavement published in 1961, the author C.S. Lewis reveals: "No one ever told me that grief was so much like fear."

Our tears flow from the lachrymal gland, which responds to the emotions of awe, pleasure, love, and, yes, sorrow. Tears are the fluid that rests in the ducts that can cause you to lose sight and can run down into your nose, all because of sorrow not joy. And, when the heart weeps, the experience goes far beyond mere liquid running into the small channels that flow into the tear sac. It is a pain that can be likened to the sound of sorrow from the mothers, fathers, family members, who have lost their loved ones in the midst of these murders and executions. "I am not afraid," wrote Lewis, "but the sensation is like being afraid: the same fluttering in the stomach, the same restlessness, the yawning. I keep on swallowing." As an African American male, I can relate to Lewis, because seemingly every day my life is at risk. I swallow grief and fear that I, or one of my brothers, our children, or mothers, could be next.

It was the sorrow of a suffering people that led ecumenical faith leaders to become the catalyst for the 1960s Civil Rights movement for a "Righteous America". These faith leaders used their sacred spaces to address their grave concerns for the least-advantaged among us. As an American society founded on a hunger and thirst for religious freedom was turning a deaf ear to the pleas of a marginalized people, certain that God's creation suffered no stratification, these like-minded humanitarians, across racial identities, were leading the charge for equality. They understood why Jesus wept, and why Mohammed, the Buddha, and many other spiritual leaders wept too.

Earlier this spring, America lost an African American male musical icon, Prince, though not at the hands of those in blue. I mostly remember him for his album Purple Rain, in particular 'When Doves Cry'. Though it is understood that these lyrics spoke to a failed relationship between two people, I purport that it speaks more to the sound of the doves. When doves cry, as they soar, it is a sorrowful song and yet in the sound we can find a message of life, hope, renewal, and peace.

Could the Prince of Peace be sending us a prophetic message that even in these moments of tragedy there is hope for better days? As we stand together through our sorrow, will we soon be able to earnestly declare that #BlackLivesMatter too?

REFLECTION II

Poverty isn't a Privilege: The White Man is Your Brother Too

Keep The Faith®

January 20, 2019

Writing to fellow clergy from Birmingham Jail in 'The Negro Is Your Brother', Reverend Dr. Martin Luther King, Jr., expressed his grave concerns about all who were poor and experiencing inequality. He said:

> *"Injustice anywhere is a threat to justice everywhere. We are caught in an inescapable network of mutuality, tied in a single garment of destiny. Whatever affects one directly, affects all indirectly."*

The world, especially America, paused on Tuesday, January 15 this year to honour Dr. King's life as a global humanitarian on what would have been his

90th birthday. The greatest birthday gift would have been to truly identify the other as our brother, sister, family. How can we really love and heal a world if we don't see our neighbours as ourselves?

Let's explore the world's events in this regard. The global crisis of the poor has affected the consciousness of both the U.K. and America. The U.K. is still being wrestled to the ground with the deal-no-deal Brexit question. Meanwhile, America has just been told that the one who was deemed the 'White Hope' is not, in fact, a traitor, and that his temper tantrum, resulting in a 35-day government shutdown has cost the U.S. economy $11 billion (according to Forbes).

This mutiny has its roots in recent political history. From the administration of former U.S. President Barack Obama to that of former U.K. Prime Minister David Cameron, few seem able to adequately identify the almost invisible group that is rapidly becoming one of the poorest in society: economically disadvantaged White children. According to the U.S. Census Bureau's latest poverty data report, published on September 12, 2018, roughly 12.8 million American children lived in poverty in 2017. Of them, 4,026,000 were White. Similarly, the Joseph Rowntree Foundation's report of December 4, 2018, indicates there are 4.1 million children living in poverty in the United Kingdom – of whom 1,271,000 are White.

In his 1935 book, Black Reconstruction, W.E.B. Du Bois introduced the concept of the psychological wage. Du Bois noted that, while White labourers received a low wage, "they were compensated in part by a sort of public and psychological wage." They were given "public deference and titles of courtesy because they were White." I'm not so sure, however, that in today's reality of Whiteness, having access to public parks, pools, and water fountains matters so much to individuals who, along with the members of non-White groups, are struggling to feed, clothe, and house their children.

The Civil Rights movement's March on Washington of August 1963 was actually the awakening of the 'Poor People's Campaign'. Reverend Dr. Martin Luther King, Jr. and his allies were going to the nation's capital to ask America to be true to the huge "promissory note" that he said had been signed when the Founding Fathers drew up the U.S. Constitution. That document had claimed to guarantee "the riches of freedom and the security of justice" for all the new republic's citizens in perpetuity, but, King said, African Americans had been excluded from that ideal for too long. "We are coming," he declared, "to engage in dramatic non-violent action, to call attention to the gulf between promise and fulfilment; to make the invisible visible." In the U.K., as in America, those who have become invisible are now forcing open the eyes of those who have forgotten them.

This year, 2019, marks 400 years since the first African immigrants – freedmen and indentured servants – arrived in Jamestown, Virginia. The Christian British colonists, who had landed there three years earlier, were now seeking to oppress the Africans, forcing them into slavery. And yet, these slaves would look for a saving grace from an individual whom they only ever saw depicted in the like image of their oppressor. That grace would eventually endow them with the power to forgive and the strength to seek civility and justice for themselves and all of humanity.

Unlike America, the U.K. has no separation of Church and state. In fact, 26 bishops sit in the House of Lords, including the Archbishop of Canterbury, Justin Welby. Recently he said of the Brexit negotiations: "The burden of proof is on those who are arguing for no deal, to show that it will not harm the poorest and most vulnerable … How we care about them and how our politics affects them is a deeply moral issue."

In the cause of bringing freedom to those invisible ones who suffer, the Church has at times been an oppressor and, in its better moments, a harbinger of liberation. For many of the Puritan settlers in America, the desire to establish a true Christian faith while maintaining an allegiance to the corruptive power of White supremacy rendered their faith in fact anti-Christian. In the case of Dr. King, his commitment to Christ the Liberator and the kingdom he proclaimed, motivated King's refusal to accept the unjust status quo, which weighed so heavily on the poor, and to act for the sake of justice.

The U.K. looks to the legacy of William Wilberforce, the abolitionist, or the current work of churches that care for the needy through food banks and debt counselling, or through organizing homes for refugee families. Selina Stone, a lecturer in political theology at St. Mellitus College, asks the pertinent question: "How will churches respond in the U.K. and in America, to those with their backs against the wall?"

Again, I ask, how can we really love and heal a world if we don't see our neighbours as ourselves? Or, in the words of Dr. King: "Injustice anywhere is a threat to justice everywhere. We are caught in an inescapable network of mutuality, tied in a single garment of destiny. Whatever affects one directly, affects all indirectly."

REFLECTION III

The Paradox of Love: President Trump's Divided States of Hate

Purposely Awakened

August 10, 2019

America is experiencing the most perilous period in its recent history as the result of the actions of President Donald Trump. On Monday morning he did step forward to speak out against the weekend's hate crimes. However, President Trump's remarks lack resonance because of the hate that has been reverberating since his stance against the Central Park Five, his ascendance in the GOP with the birther inquisition of Barack Obama, and his failure to immediately condemn the chants of "send her back" aimed at four U.S. Congresswomen for simply doing their jobs.

It remains jarring that President Trump and the leadership of the GOP demonstrate such a lack of human decency by caging children at the Mexican border and proclaiming that Baltimore is a predominately African American city where no humans should live. These hateful words are intentional verbal terrorism, designed to inflame President Trump's base and to continue to label some human beings as unworthy of being in the same race as White Americans. What is equally puzzling is the silence of the White Evangelical church, of which 81 percent of the membership support the President and believe that he has been called by God.

The blatant domestic terrorist attacks currently being exercised by White supremacists (often best known as the Ku Klux Klan and the Nazis) are embedded deeply in how the assailants understand God, practise Christianity, and see humanity. And, yet, there are social justice faith leaders who are grappling with this torture and with how to convey the message of God in these circumstances. The result today is a divided gospel.

In the New Testament Gospel of Mark 12:28-33, a scholar and scribe, out of curiosity, asks Jesus, "Which out of all the commandments is the most important?"

Jesus responds with two statements. The first is that he should: "Love the Lord your God with all your heart, your mind, your soul, and your strength." The second one is to: "Love your neighbour like you love yourself." The implication of this is very powerful because what it means is that to be authentically a follower of Jesus, I have to know how to love myself before I can love you.

I recently had a rather challenging dinner conversation with a young Jewish member of the GOP, whom I consider to be close family. He questioned why I continuously refer to this president as 'it'. He said, "You're a Christian – who believes in the same teaching as in the Torah – isn't the fundamental teaching of our faith love? If so, are you not being equally divisive in referring to Donald Trump as an 'it' and the GOP as 'them'?"

My rapid response was that human beings don't spark flames of hatred. They would not find any justification in anyone who assembles to chant 'Jews will not replace us', say that there were 'very fine people on both sides', call Mexicans rapists, and target Muslims. Those who have a soul would condemn such acrimony so that it wouldn't ignite a fire.

The Civil Rights movement wasn't driven by policy experts. It was accomplished by people who actually practised their faith in love. The movement was filled with the love of Imams and Rabbis, Catholic and Orthodox priests, Unitarians and Muslims, Baptists and Hindus, Atheists and Quakers. There were Black women frying chicken, White women making cold-cut sandwiches, gay men organizing, and lesbian women strategizing. They galvanized together to enact laws because there were racist White Americans who lacked civility. The laws had to be created to protect those whom they dehumanized with Jim Crow, and the violence of rape and torture of death.

The preaching of "whosoever shall smite thee on thy right cheek, turn to him the other also" is no longer applicable in these times. There's no longer the tolerance to mount a non-violent movement or call on foot soldiers to protest when the evidence is clear that this venom embodied in these White-skinned individuals is filled with intentional rage, injustice, and violence against everyone who isn't a pure American of 'Anglo-Saxon' descent. Yes, there are a few Blacks who are getting passes, but I learned early in life that there was no difference between house slaves and those in the field. The White supremacist groups categorically deem them all to be subhuman.

After I stepped away and reflected on my dinner conversation, I realized that my retort had caused me to depart from the most essential and guiding principle of my faith. After the race-baited massacres in El Paso, Texas, and Dayton, Ohio, by White males aged 21 and 24 in the last 48 hours, I'm now wrestling with this question – how do you continue to offer love to those who are responsible for spilling your brothers' blood on the ground?

How do, I, as a social justice intellectual and faith leader provide guidance that teaches others how to love those who persecute you and speak all manner of evil against you? How do I lean in to find similarity with those who say that they believe in the same Jesus that many non-White Americans serve? If this gospel can't unite us, especially in times like these, then what can?

Anger and love have no limits, especially when they are seeded in fear and in misappropriated religion. The Pharisees were so caught up on the rules which made up the religion that they fell short on knowing how to have a relationship with God, each other, and their neighbours.

There is no negating the reality of certain White Americans' fear of being left in poverty. According to a 2016 report by the Center on Budget and Policy Priorities, White people constitute 52 percent of those lifted from poverty by safety-net programs, while Black people make up less than a quarter of that share. When it comes to receiving medicaid, Whites make up about 43 percent of recipients, Hispanics about 30 percent, and African Americans 18 percent, with 9 percent identified as 'other'. It is obvious that Whites' concerns are valid.

However, it is unfortunate that their anger is so misappropriated. It should be directed towards the White men, like President Trump, who are more focused on their own wealth than they are on strengthening and providing economic opportunities for these White Americans.

When I awakened on Sunday morning I learned of the incident in Dayton, Ohio, where I graduated high school. My close group of friends immediately began to check on those who still reside there. We learned of several recent incidents of targeted violence in Dayton. When I learned that one of my sister-friends and her family were literally next door to where the shooting happened, I began to weep, because she's family. In our group of five, who have been friends now for over 35 years, I'm the only African American. And, yes, race shows up, because we have fluid conversations. However, what has kept our bond strong – despite the differences in our religious beliefs, sexuality, and political leanings – is love.

It was then that I realized that perhaps the answer is larger than what's in the sacred texts and man-made doctrines. The defining moments in our overcoming of hate will be drawn from what is written with love in our hearts. Maybe we can organize a healing peace-and-love march with Barack and Michelle Obama standing alongside George W. and Laura Bush? Though they had many differences, they served the United States of America, honouring a commitment to justice, equality, and love for all.

REFLECTION IV

Deliver Us from Evil: Letter to Brother Vice President Pence

June 1, 2020

Dear Vice President Pence,

Is it OK if I call you Brother Mike? I'm writing to you as a fellow Christian, which I define as being someone who believes in the teachings, words, life, death, resurrection, ascension, and second coming of Christ. I'm also writing to you as a Brown-skinned male. People like me have been classified as Negroes, Coloureds, Afro-Americans, African Americans, and Blacks. I simply deem myself to be an American.

I'm writing to you with severe pain in my heart and spirit at the state of America at this moment. I'm writing to ask of you the greatest act of kindness that one could perform as a believer in Jesus Christ: please help deliver us from evil. Please help deliver us from the evil that is racism, which is ingrained at every level of our society, as exemplified by the murder of George Floyd. Please help deliver us from the evils of division and hate – now emanating from the very heart of power – that threaten to overwhelm us.

On Friday morning when we awakened, my six-year-old son, Zayden, wanted to know, "Why is President Trump so mean? Why does he hate us?" I asked him, "Why would you say that?" He replied, "Because he tweeted that he would shoot people. That's mean. That's evil." My aim is, always, to teach him, as I was taught, about sin, but also about the forgiveness, love, grace, and mercy that we find in Jesus Christ. But my heart aches to hear an innocent child ask such a question, to witness his fear and his bewilderment.

My family of origin embraced Christianity, in spite of its role in slavery, because they were inspired by the story of Christ, the suffering servant with the power to overcome. We have held tightly to the idea that whatever hardships we may endure in life, we might dwell with him in eternity.

Much like you, Brother Mike, I am a college fraternity guy. Like you, while in college I found a deeply abiding personal relationship with Jesus as Lord. My conversion experience was also in a conservative Pentecostal church, which believes, unequivocally, that we are to 'come out from among them, be separate and sanctified holy' unto God. You and I follow the same teaching. Our churches exhort us to love the Lord with all of our being and to love our neighbours as we love ourselves. We are taught that all Christians are instructed by the Holy Scriptures to assemble together to inspire one another to love and to perform good deeds.

With all sincerity, I'm hoping that you can help me understand how our shared belief system aligns with the actions of U.S. President Donald Trump, the man that you stand next to, uphold, and honour. I am by no means am judging you. I'm trying to gain clarity and wisdom. President Trump's many and often self-professed sins (adultery, misogyny, greed, lying, vanity) are a matter of public record. And now, at this crucial moment for our country, he tweets vile and painful words of division and seems to degrade others without human compassion. He even appears to incite violence. Where is the love? Where are the good deeds?

I have wrestled, much like Jacob, to try to understand all of this.

Each night as I put Zayden to bed, we pray the prayer that Jesus taught his disciples. Without hesitation, when we get to "and, deliver us from evil" Zayden says it loudest and with authority. I asked him why. He said, "Because I know that God can protect us from evil." I always remind him that we, as God's believers, must ensure that our hearts are filled with his love — that his will can be done on earth through us, as it is in heaven, if we trust love and give love in return.

I believe that you are a man who wholeheartedly believes in Jesus Christ as Lord and stands representing him. What would you suggest that I tell Zayden and other little boys and girls with Brown tones of skin about the President's words, actions, and behaviours? Should I tell them that there is a defining line in what we believe that is different based on race? Do I try to explain that non-White Evangelical Christians won't be able to enter paradise through the same pearly gates? Maybe there's a back door for some, a lower level, because of an unequal salvation? Or, perchance, there's a difference in how Jesus loves me versus you?

We really need your help, Brother Mike – America needs you. What we are seeing every day right now isn't love. What we are hearing from the White House isn't love. So, I'm sending this as a heartfelt plea, asking you to please, help us all to be delivered from this evil.

Your brother in Christ, Keith

The Reverend Professor Keith Magee
The Berachah Church, Boston, Massachusetts, U.S.A.
Newcastle University, Newcastle upon Tyne, U.K.

REFLECTION V

The Truth: It's Sometimes Black and White

The Seattle Medium

August 24, 2020

Before I belong to a race, party, or gender, I belong to God. I believe that we're all made in the image of God. As a follower of Jesus, I'm committed to the greatest of his commandments: to love the Lord my God with all my heart, soul, and mind and to love my neighbour.

America has long suffered from the sin of racism. Race is a social construct that was designed to create powerlessness, division, and fear amongst those who had been enslaved and deemed soulless. Today, as the election approaches, we stand at what I hope will be a key turning point in history. In the midst of the terrible division, sickness, fear, and grief we have experienced in recent months, we have a real chance to unite all America's people in the causes of civility, healing, hope, and justice. To do this, we must remove President Trump from office.

On August 19, Kamala Harris, an American-born, Jamaican-Indian United States senator, became the first woman of colour to be the vice-presidential nominee to a major U.S. political party. As we celebrate this important moment, let us also rejoice in the myriad things that make us all so different and yet all so alike, all so unique, and yet all God's children.

Although 60.3% of Americans are White, and 52.9% of them are women, no White woman has ever been president. However, it is now crucial that White women are galvanized to vote overwhelmingly for a male Democrat to take that office and perhaps pass the mantle on to a Black woman – in what would be another historic first. I believe that, as running mates, Joe Biden and Kamala Harris embody the unity and solidarity we all long for. Women understand perhaps more than anyone our country's need for togetherness right now. But we have to ensure that all women feel part of our movement, and that must include White women.

I am a Black man for whom many pivotal moments in life have come through White women believing in me. Marie Bennett hired me, in spite of my dyslexia, to work on a project of federal significance. Caroline Cracraft, whom I adore as my British mum, is the reason why I have a life in the United Kingdom. It was a 'Karen' who gave me courage to soar beyond where I was eight years ago and to flourish, fulfilling what I thought at the time were unrealistic expectations.

My first 'granddaughter,' Eleanor Irene, was born on July 7. She happens to be White. She's the daughter of my Jordan, who came to work for me as an intern in 2009. Jordan had lost both of her parents and was navigating her life as a beautiful soul without them. Ever since, I have loved her, and her growing family, as my own, because that is what they are.

I want our Democratic party to reflect all their hopes, needs, and aspirations, just as it must those of their Black sisters and friends.

I am so grateful to the White women who did and do understand the call of justice and equality within their hearts and souls. Many have stood beside us in the fight for equal rights, including Juliette Morgan and NAACP founders Mary White Ovington and Florence Kelley. Countless White women played an active role in recent anti-racism demonstrations, not just in the U.S., but all over the world. They give me hope.

But I am also afraid. We are in a daunting place. Our opponents may outnumber us in some of the states we need to carry, and they may well not play fair. I am worried for the America that our ancestors died to build, where our parents endured so much for us to have fairer opportunities and where is so much still to overcome. I am worried that as we rejoice in Biden's choice of a Black woman as his running mate, we may forget to open our arms to the White women whose support we so badly need. We must do everything in our power to maximize the impact of the Biden-Harris symbol of unity and hope. We must ensure that White women of every age and socio-economic group also see themselves reflected in our messaging, our campaigning, and in those whom we ask to endorse us.

So here is my prayer, my Lord. Let this be a moment to heal the soul of America with love, compassion, equality, and dignity. Let us be careful not to create another divide, but instead build a bridge to our collective humanity. Let us not make this a polarizing moment but let us be all-inclusive and united. Let us inspire every single voter to join us, whatever their gender, and whatever the colour of their skin happens to be. Let us beat Trump together.

A CALL TO ACTION

Everything in this book has been written to inspire us towards a call to action – believing that if each of us performs all or even some of these actions, we will leave the world better than we've found it. So, let's together commit ourselves to:

Recalibrating the scales of justice – our nations have not treated all their children fairly. Many souls have been denied justice simply because of the colour of their skin. None of us can live in peace until there is justice for all of us, all the time. Change will be required, but this cannot be beyond us.

Creating brave spaces in which we can face up to the past and embrace the future – we need, now more than ever, to come together instead of moving further apart. There are many ways and places in which we can do this. We can do it in our homes, schools, town halls, community centres, places of worship, out in nature, online, and in our great centres of democracy at state and national level. We can talk together, walk together, work on community projects together, plan together, dream together, pray together.

Acting with courage – it won't be easy to face up to uncomfortable truths about our history, our collective memories, and ourselves, and to work out how we can recontextualize the vestiges of the past so that they tell more authentic stories. Nor is it easy to truly seek to listen to and understand another person's feelings and point of view, but I believe that God will give us the courage we need to achieve this if we are brave enough to open our hearts.

Identifying common ground – today we live in a society that is divided along so many lines. It is not just questions of race, religion, and politics that separate us, but also gender, sexuality, wealth, place, how we define morality, even how we define truth. And yet, if we look for them in earnest, I am convinced that we will also find countless things that unite us. We will discover many issues on which we can agree that, at the very least, we all want to move towards a better, less polarized future for our children.

Celebrating our collective humanity – once we begin to break down the barriers between us, we will be rewarded with glimpses of our common humanity. We must plant those precious seeds of 'alikeness', nurture them with love, and watch them bloom into a more harmonious way of being with one another.

Building a beloved community – when you look at 'the other' and see their soul, you begin to find ways to love them. Jesus asked each of us to love our neighbour. In our modern, global community, everyone is our neighbour. We will need big hearts, but we can do this, together. After all, what is the alternative?

The Afterthought

A Prayer for the Soul of a Nation

Democrats Abroad, Global Black Caucus:
Black Lives Matter Vigil

June 2, 2020

I hope that these seminal writings have enabled you to hear the prophetic voice that we have within one another. I hope that they give way to you seeing justice through your own voice.

And, more than anything, I leave you with this prayer.

Creator of all things, I pause in this moment to offer 'A Prayer for the Soul of our Nation'.

"My country 'tis of thee, Sweet land of liberty, Of thee I sing."[1]

"God of our weary years, God of our silent tears, Thou who has brought us thus far on the way, Thou who has by Thy might led us into the light, Keep us forever in the path, we pray."[2]

In the sacred Christian text, in Genesis 2, it says that you, God, formed man of the dust of the ground, and breathed into his nostrils the breath of life; human beings (male and female) became living souls. So, when we die our bodies return to dust. But while we're 'alive' we all have our souls – we are all breathing life and with that life comes responsibility.

I pray that the breath of God will breathe on the soul of our nation – that America might truly honour, love, and protect the Souls of Black Folks. May America truly come to understand the prophetic utterances of W.E.B Du Bois. He saw the never-ending struggle of the colour line. He addressed the concern that over half the world would be denied the right of sharing and obtaining the opportunities and privileges of 'modern' civilization, all because of that divisive colour line.

May the world someday understand why Du Bois referred to the term 'double consciousness', perhaps taken from Ralph Waldo Emerson's The

Transcendentalist and Fate. This notion of 'double consciousness' means that Black people must have two fields of vision at all times. We must be conscious of how we view ourselves, as well as being conscious of how the world views us, so that we might live and breathe to experience God's amazing grace.

It is grace that has brought us through the many dangerous toils and snares we have already endured. 'Twas grace. Yahweh's amazing grace. Not presidents, politics, or rhetoric, but God's grace. It was grace. Not the White House or some club house but the Creator's grace ...

What we, the world, America, needs is not to be 'great'. We need God's amazing grace – to answer the call of those crying out for the liberty and justice that's owed to all.

Grace is the only thing that can transition the hearts of men and women to lead us on. I pray for God's grace to cause us to hold this truth to be self-evident: all men are created equal. I call on God's amazing grace so that justice may "roll down like water and righteousness like a mighty stream!"[3]

145

The Reverend Dr. Martin Luther King, Jr. said that there is a deep understanding of the need for agape. A love that is concerned with going the extra mile to ensure the well-being of others. King believed in a better world, but in order to attain his vision he argued that we must first face our fears and then master these fears through love, faith, and courage.

We also need courage and strength to face each day in the truth that there are Black lives amongst us that don't matter to some. We need courage to see the poor amongst us, regardless of their race or religion. We need courage to see the other, our brothers and sisters, as ourselves. We need courage, wrapped in strength, to hope for better days. Strength to have faith in what we can't see, but a hope that is possible and causes our souls to rise. And, and most of all – the strength to stand in love for all of God's children, no matter skin colour, heritage, language, sexuality, religion – no matter the difference.

Give us the courage to stand, for our souls to decree – so that our message resounds in America and around the world – that we are broken as a people, but that love can guide us.

Give us courage to truly be who we are, who we are becoming, not a people fighting against each other but standing shoulder to shoulder together in harmony.

As global citizens, we have work to do – to get the world, America, to bring us to "courage". May the words of Coretta Scott King reverberate through our spirits, not so that we be discouraged but so that we realize that:

> *"Struggle is a never-ending process. Freedom is never really won. You earn it and win it in every generation. You don't finally win a state of freedom that is protected forever. It doesn't work that way."*

Our world, America, needs healing for its never-ending struggle to redeem its soul.

And, it is my prayer that you will be inspired by these writings to see that we are the ones to do it. We need to stand together as a people of common struggles, even when we have polar-opposite beliefs. Some Buddhists and Jews, some Christians and Muslims, some Jedis and Atheists.

May we have the courage to overcome fear, that we might love the other as ourselves. May the pureness of our hearts cause us to understand that it is required of all of us "to do justly and to love mercy, and to walk humbly with our God".[4] There is no provision in the Bible towards a difference in our politics, race, or religion. When we open our hearts to love, we have a great chance of embracing a beloved soul whose longings, ideologies, and hopes are diametrically opposed to ours. But know that:

> *"There is no fear in love; but perfect love casteth out fear: because fear hath torment. He that feareth is not made perfect in love."*[5]

We must bravely look towards a brighter future tomorrow, for generations to come, that we might assure our children and our children's children that there is a U.S. Constitution that truly embodies a more perfect Union. That truly establishes justice to ensure domestic tranquillity. A Constitution that truly provides for the common defences, promotes the general welfare, and secures the blessings of liberty for us and for posterity.

We have some hard days ahead, but we can do this.

I believe, dear God, that what's critical to this moment in history is for those who understand both the soul and the U.S. Constitution to also understand our duty, our obligation to all of your children – especially those with Brown skin tones.

May we live beyond the simple question of Plato's Republic and create a just city. May we know justice as a virtue for all human beings in a democracy.

Maybe the goddess Themis, who orders nature, as she stands holding the scales of justice, bring us to a lifetime of justice that is critical within a democracy.

Hear my plea Divine, so that someday soon we can truly "Lift every voice and sing, Till earth and heaven ring, Ring with the harmonies of liberty." May the day come when our rejoicing will truly "Rise, high as the listening skies", resounding "loud as the rolling sea".

May someday all Americans cry out together "Shadowed beneath thy hand, May we forever stand" – as a united people, one nation, under God indivisible. And then we can all be "True to our God, True to our native land."

Hear our prayer, Creator,

Hear our prayers, The Force,

Hear our prayers, The Mother of Eternity,

Hear our prayers, The Great Sovereign One.

And, it is so.

Acknowledgements

My journey with this book, beyond transcribing my thoughts onto my computer screen, is the manifestation of the thoughtfulness and support of so many. I certainly must thank Karen Pritzker for the push to "get the book out", Joanne Clay for her editorial genius and guidance, and the unwavering support of my personal team: Sharon White, Nkemakolam Anyanwu, Ivan Garcia Cuellar, and Beverly Jackson – who is an anchor, rock, and sure foundation. I'm eternally grateful for two prescient women who continue to nurture me in the rules and protocols of politics, Dianne Wilkerson and Lynnie Powell – who frequently reminds me that "you've gotta love Black people to fight for them".

There are prophets amongst us whose voices transcend within the public sphere and their bodies of work strengthen my awareness of ethics, faith, policy, and meaning – the late Samuel DeWitt Proctor, my guiding light; along with Marvin McMickle, Lawrence Carter, Marie Bennett, Carol Moseley Braun, Julia Stasch, Jackie Jenkins Scott, Katherine Kennedy, Peter

Edelman (a living legend whose heart for poverty and policy awakens), and Lonnie Bunch – whose gifts for preserving heritage, curating culture, and dispersing knowledge are framing the future. A special shout out to Tonya Veasey for listening and helping me to merge the practicalities of faith and policy. To all my colleagues at University College London, Black Britain and Beyond, and Newcastle University, I'm grateful for the place of intellectual consideration in scholarship and applied practice – with special acknowledgement to Simon Cane, Emma Bryant, Bryan Bonaparte, Julie Saunders, Helen Berry and Richard Clay.

My family by blood and love, Ashley, E.L., Brittany, Che, Morgan, Bruce, Bernard, Jordan, Christian, Carolyn, Ariell, Christopher, Michael, Brianna, Julia, Joel, Teddy, and Shaun – thank you all for being your authentic selves. Thank you to my brothers of Kappa Alpha Psi, especially my LBs Dwayne, Wayne, Paul, and Tony, along with Andre, Enrique, Jermaine and Ricalder. To my brothers from my other mothers, Joe, Melvin, Richard, Garrett and Freddie Lee – whose praying has brought me through many dangerous toils and snares. My sister-friends Carla, Rutina, Patti, Eryca, Alisha, Kim, and Norma – whose silence speaks volumes. There's a depth of gratitude engraved in my heart to my best friend and confidant, Lenny Lopez, who understands ON. I'm forever grateful to my British mum, Caroline Cracraft, who opened the portal for my life in the United Kingdom. Thank you to the one who birthed me from a womb filled with love and who guides me like the north star, my mother Barbara Reynolds. And, to my father, the late Alvin Magee, who gave me wings to soar beyond the bayou of Louisiana into this surreal place.

For the dyslexic adults and children, this is a nod for you to remember that you can. To the undergirding strength and prayers that keep me grounded and those in which I'm humbled to serve, The Berachah Family @The Living Room, where I'm not a normal pastor, they're not a normal church — and our committed Executive Pastor, Cyntoria Grant, stands alongside me, I thank you. And, to you, the reader, the citizen, none of this is important without your picking up this manuscript to read – for you, I'm grateful.

About the Author

Keith Magee is a public intellectual, theologian, and social justice scholar. He is Chair and Professor of Social Justice at Newcastle University School of History, Classics and Archaeology and serves as Senior Advisor to the Chancellor and Deputy Vice Chancellor. He is Senior Fellow in Culture and Justice, University College London where he is the principal investigator for Black Britain and Beyond. He founded the Social Justice Institute in 2014 while in post at Boston University - it remains the hub for his independent work and research. He is also the Lead Pastor at The Berachah Church, which has a virtual global presence.

Having trained as an economist and in theology, at Grace Bible College and Harvard. His work reflects on the Ten Commandments as 'public policies', thereby exploring how they inform society through belief, culture, and economic and social justice.

One of his greatest accomplishments was serving for five years as the founding director of the National

Public Housing Museum in Chicago, Illinois. He successfully initiated and led a $13 million capital campaign for the museum, which is committed to being a living cultural experience on social justice and human rights, illuminating the power of place.

He currently serves as an advisor for the forthcoming Biden-Harris administration on racial inequality, having served as an advisor to the campaign. He served as Senior Religious Affairs Advisor with the Obama for America 2008 and 2012 campaigns, subsequently working alongside the Obama administration's Faith Based Initiative. Previously, he served as Co-Chair of the Massachusetts Council of Chaplains in State Institutions for Governor Deval Patrick. Additionally, he sits on the board of directors of the Congressional Black Caucus Foundation where he's Chair of both the Endowment and Nominations committees. He is also a Trustee of Facing History and Ourselves and the Co-Chair of Black Britain and Beyond. He is a Fellow of the Royal Society of Arts and was inducted into Morehouse College's Martin Luther King Jr. Collegium of Scholars. He is a life member of Kappa Alpha Psi Fraternity, Inc.

Additionally, he is passionate about providing humanitarian aid to children and families throughout the world. He is currently leading the effort to open the first public library in Kampala, Uganda, that will provide children with access to over 20,000 books.

As a dyslexic, he has secured more than $15 million to develop programmes and initiatives that advocate for and support dyslexic people globally. His efforts have led him to co-create the Multicultural Initiative at Yale University Center for Dyslexia and Creativity, and to co-found the Urban Teachers Masters of Education Residency Training Program at Saint Joseph's University.

Reverend Professor Magee's body of work has seen him awarded with distinctions and the support of the MacArthur, Ford, and Seedlings foundations. He is an internationally sought-after speaker and frequently features as a columnist and op-ed opinion contributor on issues of social justice, politics, race, and religion both in the United Kingdom and United States. He and his six-year-old son, Zayden, live between London, England and Boston, Massachusetts.

BIBLIOGRAPHY

Books

Allen, Richard. *The Life, Experience, and Gospel Labours of the Rt. Rev. Richard Allen.* Philadelphia: Martin & Boden, Printers, 1833.

Aristotle. *Nicomachean Ethics.* Translated and with an introduction by Martin Ostwald. New York: Macmillan, 1962.

Berger, Roger. *Surviving the Holocaust: A Life Course Perspective.* New York: Taylor & Francis, 2010.

Bunch, Lonnie G. *A Fool's Errand: Creating the National Museum of African American History and Culture During the Age of Bush, Obama, and Trump.* Washington, D.C.: Smithsonian, 2019.

Calaresu, Melissa; Rubies, Joan-Pau; de Vivo, Filippo. *Exploring Cultural History Essays in Honour of Peter Burke.* London: Routledge, 2010.

Clinton, Hillary R. *What Happened.* New York: Simon and Schuster, 2017.

Conrad, Edward (ed). *The Constitution of the United States, with Case Summaries.* 9th edition. New York: Barnes and Noble Books, 1972.

Cowell, Edward Byles (ed.). *The Jātaka: Or, Stories of the Buddha's Former Births, Cambridge*: University Press, 1895.

Doddridge, Philip. *The Rise and Progress of Religion in the Soul.* Whitefish, Montana: Kessinger, 2003 (first published 1822).

Du Bois, W.E.B. *Black Reconstruction in America: An Essay Toward a History of the Part Which Black Folk Played in the Attempt to Reconstruct Democracy in America, 1860–1880*. New York: Harcourt, Brace, 1935.

Du Bois, W.E.B. *The Souls of Black Folk*. Chicago: A.C. McClurg & Co., 1903.

Duster, Michelle. Ida in Her Own Words: *The Timeless Writings of Ida B. Wells from 1893*. Lansing, Illinois: Benjamin Williams Publishing, 2008.

Eddo-Lodge, Reni. *Why I'm No Longer Talking to White People About Race*. London: Bloomsbury, 2017.

Edelman, Peter. *Not A Crime to Be Poor: The Criminalization of Poverty in America*. New York: The New Press, 2017.

Farrar, Reginald. *The Life of Frederic William, Sometime Dean of Canterbury*. New York: Thomas Y. Crowell and Publishers, 1904.

Fierman, Morton C. *Leap of Action: Ideas in the Theology of Abraham Joshua Heschel*. New York: Lanham, 1990.

Frankfurt, Harry. *On Inequality*. Princeton, New Jersey: Princeton University Press, 2015.

Friedland, Michael. *Lift Up Your Voice Like a Trumpet: White Clergy and the Civil Rights and Antiwar Movements*. Chapel Hill, North Carolina: University of North Carolina Press, 1998.

Gordon, Linda. *The Second Coming of the KKK: The Ku Klux Klan of the 1920s and the American Political Tradition*. New York: Liveright, 2017.

Heschel, Abraham Joshua. *Moral Grandeur and Spiritual Audacity: Essays*. New York: Macmillan, 1997.

Heschel, Susannah. *"Theological Affinities in the Writings of Abraham Joshua Heschel and Martin Luther King, Jr."* The Rabbinical Assembly, 1998.

Holy Bible, English Standard Version Study Bible. Crossway, 2011.

Holy Bible, New International Version. Zondervan Publishing House, 1984.

Kaplan, Edward. *Abraham Joshua Heschel: Prophetic Witness*. London: Yale University Press, 1998.

King, Coretta Scott; Reynolds, Barbara A. *My Life, My Love, My Legacy*. New York: Henry Holt & Co., 2017.

King Jr., Martin Luther. *Strength to Love*. Cleveland: Collins + World, 1977.

Kivel, Paul. *Uprooting Racism: How White People Can Work for Racial Justice*. Philadelphia and British Columbia: New Society Publishers, 1996.

Knox, Robert. *The Races of Man: A Fragment*. Philadelphia: Lea and Blanchard, 1850.

Lewis, C.S. *A Grief Observed*. Grand Rapids, Michigan: Zondervan, 1989.

Lindqvist, Sven. *Exterminate All the Brutes: One Man's Odyssey into the Heart of Darkness and the Origins of European Genocide*. New York: The New Press, 1996.

McMickle, Marvin. *Where Have All the Prophets Gone: Reclaiming Prophetic Preaching in America*. Cleveland: The Pilgrim Press, 2006.

Moore, Leonard J. *Citizen Klansmen: The Ku Klux Klan in Indiana, 1921–1928*. Chapel Hill: University of North Carolina, 1991.

Nash, Gary B. *Forging Freedom: The Formation of Philadelphia's Black Community, 1720–1840*. Cambridge, Massachusetts: Harvard University Press, 1991.

Pepper, William. *An Act of State: The Execution of Martin Luther King*. London: Verso, 2003.

Phillips, Layli. *The Womanist Reader*. New York: Routledge, 2006.

Plato. Plato's The Republic. New York: Books, Inc., 1943.

Pogrebin, Letty. *Deborah, Golda & Me: Being Female and Jewish in America*. New York: Crown, 1991.

Rawls, John. *A Theory of Justice*. Cambridge, Massachusetts: Harvard University Press, 1971.

Sandel, Michael J. Justice: *What is the Right Thing to Do*. New York: Farrar Straus Giroux, 2009.

Schneier, Marc. *Shared Dreams: Martin Luther King Jr. and the Jewish Community*. Woodstock, Vermont: Jewish Lights Publishing, 1999.

Thayer, Joseph H. *The New Thayer's Greek-English Lexicon of the New Testament*. Peabody, Massachusetts: Hendrickson, 1981.

The Book of Resolutions of The United Methodist Church. Nashville, Tennessee: United Methodist Publishing House, 2016.

The Torah, *The Five Books of Moses, the New Translation of the Holy Scriptures According to the Traditional Hebrew Text*. Philadelphia: The Jewish Publication Society, 1999.

Truth, Sojourner, Ain't I A Woman? (Penguin Great Ideas), *New York: Penguin*, 2020.

Truth, Sojourner, The Narrative of Sojourner Truth: A Northern

Slave (1850), New York: Dover Publications 1997.

Walker, Alice. *In search of Our Mother's Garden*. New York: Harcourt, 1983.

Washington, Booker T., Du Bois, W.E.B. (et al). *The Negro Problem: The Talented Tenth*. New York: J. Pott & Company, 1903.

Acts, Laws, and Policies

Hansard. "Slave Trade Abolition Bill," Vol 8, cc717–22. February 10, 1807.

Henry, Natasha L. "Slavery Abolition Act." Encyclopaedia Britannica, July 25, 2020.

The Civil Rights Act of 1964 (Pub.L. 88–352, 78 Stat. 241: enacted July 2, 1964.)

The Violent Crime Control and Law Enforcement Act of 1994 (H.R. 3355, Pub.L. 103–322: passed August 21, 1994.)

The Voting Rights Act of 1965 (Pub. L. 89-110, 79 Stat. 437: enacted August 6, 1965.)

U. S. Constitution

Journals, Magazines, and Newspapers

Boston Magazine

Bustle

Buzzfeed News

Center for American Progress

Evening Standard

NPR

Photochemistry and Photobiology

Purposely Awake

Seattle Medium

The Afro-American

The Atlantic

The London Economic

The New York Times

The New Yorker

The Sentencing Project

The Tennessee Journal On The Hill

The Wall Street Journal

The Washington Post

The Watch Tower

Theories of Psychology

Timeline.com

Films

Griffith, D.W. *The Clansman – The Birth of a Nation*. United States: David W. Griffith Corp., 1915.

Kempner, Aviva. Rosenwald: *The Remarkable Story of a Jewish Partnership with African American Communities*. Ciesla Foundation (http://rosenwaldfilm.org/rosenwald/): 2018.

Lemmons, Kassi. *Eve's Bayou*. United States: Chubb Co Film and

Addis-Wechsler, 1997.

Parker, Nate. *The Birth of a Nation*. United States: Mandalay Pictures, 2016.

Spielberg, Steven. *The Color Purple*. United States: Amblin Entertainment, 1985.

Music

Gamble, Kenny; Huff, Leon. "The Sound of Philadelphia (*Soul Train* theme song)." Philadelphia: Philadelphia International Records, 1973.

McCall, David; Dorough, Bob. *"Schoolhouse Rock!*: Lolly, Lolly, Lolly, Get Your Adverbs Here." New York: Scholastic Rock, Inc., ABC, 1974.

McCall, David; Ahrens, Lynn. *"Schoolhouse Rock!*: The Preamble." New York: Scholastic Rock, Inc., ABC, 1974.

Prince. "Purple Rain: When Doves Cry." Warner Brothers, 1984.

Redding, Otis. "Respect." New York: Atlantic Records, 1967.

Endnotes

Chapter One

1   Dindal, Mark. *Chicken Little.* Buena Vista Pictures, 2005.

2   *Holy Bible*, New International Version, Matthew 24:6. Zondervan Publishing House, 1984.

3   Thayer, Joseph H. *The New Thayer's Greek-English Lexicon of the New Testament.* Peabody, Massachusetts: Hendrickson, 1981.

4   Brown, DeNeen L. "The Preacher Who used Christianity to Revive the Ku Klux Klan." *The Washington Post*, April 10, 2018.

5   Moore, Leonard J. Citizen Klansmen: *The Ku Klux Klan in Indiana*, 1921–1928. Chapel Hill, North Carolina: University of North Carolina, 1991.

6   Pepper, William. *An Act of State: The Execution of Martin Luther King.* London: Verso, 2003. Nash, Gary B. *Forging Freedom: The Formation of Philadelphia's Black Community*, 1720–1840. Cambridge, Massachusetts: Harvard University Press, 1991.

7   Allen, Richard. *The Life, Experience, and Gospel Labours of the Rt. Rev. Richard Allen.* Philadelphia: Martin & Boden Printers, 1833, p. 13.

8   The laying on of hands in the Black Church is an act of touching in agreement and encouragement in faith. It is both a symbolic and formal method of invoking the Holy Spirit to have divine will of those who are "touching" and praying in agreement. This is a long-held tradition dating back to the New Testament, in which this symbolic gesture

was associated with Christ healing the sick (Luke 4:40) and, after his ascension, the receiving of the Holy Spirit (Acts 8:14–19).

9   McMickle, Marvin. *Where Have All the Prophets Gone: Reclaiming Prophetic Preaching in America.* Cleveland: The Pilgrim Press, 2006.

10   The sound bites from Jeremiah Wright came from two of his sermons: "The Day of Jerusalem's Fall", delivered on September 16, 2001 and "Confusing God and Government", delivered on April 13, 2003. Both of these messages were delivered long before Barack Obama was a U.S. Senator, therefore well in advance of his seeking the democratic presidential nomination. This sermon content, while some may consider it to be contentious, is typical within Black prophetic preaching. It is believed to speak truth to power.

11   Obama, Barack. "A More Perfect Union." *The Wall Street Journal*, March 18, 2008.

12   Kuhn, David Paul. "Exit polls: How Obama won." *Politico*, November 5, 2008.

13   "Make America Great Again" (MAGA) was a campaign slogan which was popularized by Donald Trump in his successful 2016 presidential bid. He revived and adapted it from a similar slogan, "Let's Make America Great Again", used by Ronald Reagan in his successful 1980 presidential bid. The terminology has long been held within American politics to be divisive. Marissa Melton reported it as coded racism: "Is 'Make America Great Again' Racist?" *Voice of America*, August 31, 2017. Kristen Jordan Shamus described it as a symbol of hate: "MAGA hats: Trump campaign swag or symbols of hate?" *Detroit Free Press*, January 24, 2019. Robin Abcarian wrote "MAGA hats and blackface are different forms of expression, but they share a certain unfortunate DNA." *Los*

Angeles Times, February 5, 2019.

14 Bailey, Sarah Pulliam. "White evangelicals voted overwhelmingly for Donald Trump, exit polls show." *Washington Post*, November 9, 2016.

15 Elving, Ron. "What Is A Nationalist In The Age Of Trump?" *NPR Analysis*, October 24, 2018.

16 Cowell, Edward Byles (ed.). "The Jātaka: Or, Stories of the Buddha's Former Births." Cambridge: Cambridge University Press, 1895, VI. No. 322.

17 "Fate/Grand Order" is a turn-based tactical role-playing game. The player takes the role of "Master" and commands a group of individuals called "Servants", who are typically historical, literary, and mythological figures from various cultures. The premise is based on the Chaldea Security Organization in 2015. The Organization draws on experts of both the magical and mundane fields to observe the future of mankind for possible extinction events. Humanity's survival seems assured for the next century – until the verdict suddenly changes, and now eradication of the species awaits at the end of 2016. The cause is unknown, but appears to be linked with the Japanese town of Fuyuki and the events of 2004 during the Fifth Holy Grail War. After a series of occurrences, the survivors must decide the ultimate fate of human history. The leader of the survivors must make some grave decisions and sacrifices that either will make him a saviour or a destroyer.

18 Hawkins, Derek; Fritz, Angela. "Trump's spiritual adviser called for 'all satanic pregnancies to miscarry.' It was a metaphor, she says." *Washington Post*, January 26, 2020.

19 Reverend Wright at the National Press Club, Transcript. *The New York Times*, April 28, 2008.

Chapter Two

1   Aristotle. *Politics*, Book 3, section 1282b.

2   Sandel, Michael. Justice: *What is the Right Thing to Do*. New York: Penguin, 2010.

3   Aristotle, *Politics*, Book 3, section 1282b.

4   Sandel, p. 193.

5   Black Lives Matter (BLM) is an international activist movement, originating in the African American community, that campaigns against violence and systemic racism towards Black people. BLM regularly protests police killings of Black people and broader issues of racial profiling, police brutality, and racial inequality in the United States criminal justice system. In 2013, the movement began with the use of the hashtag #BlackLivesMatter on social media, after the acquittal of George Zimmerman in the fatal shooting of African American teen Trayvon Martin. Black Lives Matter became nationally recognized for its street demonstrations following the 2014 deaths of two African Americans: Michael Brown, resulting in protests and unrest in Ferguson, and Eric Garner in New York City. The originators of the hashtag and call to action, Alicia Garza, Patrisse Cullors, and Opal Tometi, expanded their project into a national network of over 30 local chapters between 2014 and 2016. The overall Black Lives Matter movement, however, is a decentralized network and has no formal hierarchy. Since the Ferguson protests, participants in the movement have demonstrated against the deaths of numerous other African Americans by police actions or while in police custody.

6   Kivel, Paul. *Uprooting Racism: How White People Can Work for Racial Justice*. Philadelphia and British Columbia: New Society Publishers, 1996, p. 17.

7   Lindqvist, Sven. *Exterminate All the Brutes: One Man's Odyssey into the Heart of Darkness and the Origins of European Genocide*. New York: The New Press, 1996, Chapter 4.

8   "Structure and Function Of The Skin – Wound Care Education." *CliniMed*, January 31, 2019.

9   King Jr., Martin Luther. "I Have a Dream" speech. Washington, D.C., August 28, 1963.

10 Plato. *Apology of Socrates*, 30a–b.

11 Kaufmann, Kohler. "Immortality of the Soul." www.jewishencyclopedia.com. Archived from the original on December 20, 2016.

12 *ESV Study Bible*. English Standard Version, Crossway, 2011.

13 Genzlinger, Neil. "Noel Ignatiev, 78, Persistent Voice Against White Privilege, Dies." *New York Times*, November 14, 2019. Written by Noel Ignatiev in 1995, *How the Irish Became White* is among a group of books that have been foundational to what became known as whiteness studies, a field that examines the structures that produce White privilege.

14 The Civil Rights Act of 1964 (Pub.L. 88–352, 78 Stat. 241, enacted July 2, 1964.)

Chapter Three

1   "Women Klan Members Reveal Family Life." *New York Times*, October 1, 1922, http://www.proquest.com.

2   *Eve's Bayou* is a 1997 American drama written and directed by Kasi Lemmons, who made her directorial debut with this film. Samuel L. Jackson served as a producer, and starred in the film with Lisa Nicole Carson, Jurnee Smollett, Lynn Whitfield, Debbi Morgan, and Megan Good. Eve Batiste, a 10-year-old girl, lives in a prosperous Creole-American

community in Louisiana with her younger brother Poe and her older sister Cisely in the 1960s. Their parents are Roz and Louis, a well-respected doctor in Louisiana's "coloured" community who claims descent from the French aristocrat who founded the town of Eve's Bayou. One night after a raucous party, Eve accidentally witnesses her father having sex with a family friend. However, Cisely, who has a very affectionate relationship with her father, convinces Eve that she misinterpreted an innocent moment. The unreliability of memory and observation remain important themes throughout the film.

3   D.W. Griffith's *Birth of a Nation*, released on February 8, 1915, was a landmark silent film. The film was released in its first month under its actual title, The Clansman, after the name of the book from which the screenplay was developed. It was America's first feature-length motion picture. During its unprecedented three hours, Griffith popularized countless film-making techniques that remain central to the art today. The film provides a highly subjective history of the Civil War, Reconstruction, and the rise of the Ku Klux Klan. Most alarming was its explicit racism against Black Americans, causing it to be one of the most offensive films ever released.

4   Lehr, Dick. "The Racist Legacy of Woodrow Wilson." *The Atlantic,* November 27, 2017.

5   Feminism "advocates for women's rights on the grounds of political, social, and economic equality to men," according to Google's dictionary. I'll admit this definition leaves something to be desired; modern feminism, for example, acknowledges more than two genders, so the movement is not just about advancing women. See "7 Things The Word 'Feminist' Does NOT Mean." *Bustle,* July 5, 2016 (www.bustle.com/articles/170721-7-things-the-word-feminist-does-not-mean).

6   *Watcher on the Tower*, September 15, 1923, 12. This was published by the Seattle Klan.

7   An apotheosis actually means deification.

8   John Calvin (French: Jean Cauvin) was born on July 10, 1509, in Picardy, France, and died on May 27, 1564, in Geneva, Switzerland. A theologian and ecclesiastical statesman, he was the leading French Protestant Reformer and the most important figure in the second generation of the Protestant Reformation. The Calvinist form of Protestantism is widely thought to have had a major impact on the formation of the modern world. Calvinists departed from the Roman Catholic Church in the 16th century. Calvinists differ from Lutherans on the real presence of Christ in the Eucharist, theories of worship, and the use of God's law for believers, among other things.

9   Susan B. Anthony and Frederick Douglass were close friends and allies for both abolition and women's suffrage since the mid-1840s. After the Civil War the relationship was strained when Frederick Douglass adopted a gradualist position and wanted to concentrate on rights for African Americans first. Douglass feared that trying to achieve universal suffrage all at once would be too difficult. Meanwhile Anthony feared that progressing in steps would inevitably stop short of full universal suffrage and viewed Douglass's stance as a betrayal of the cause. This statement was made in 1866 at a meeting in response to Douglass pushing for Anthony to support the 15th Amendment without the inclusion of women as a protected class.

10 Gordon, Linda. *The Second Coming of the KKK: The Ku Klux Klan of the 1920s and the American Political Tradition.* New York: Liveright, 2017.

11 Gordon, Linda. "How Women In The KKK Were

Instrumental To Its Rise." *Buzzfeed News*, August 15, 2017.

12 Smith, Laura. "One Woman's effort to mix Klan-style Hatred with Wholesome Christian Values." *Timeline.com*, January 10, 2018.

13 Phillips, Layli. "Womanism: On Its Own," Introduction, *The Womanist Reader*. New York and Abingdon: Routledge, 2006, p. xix.

14 Walker, Alice. *In search of Our Mother's Garden*. New York: Harcourt, 1983, p. xi.

15 Walker, 2005, p. xii.

16 *The Birth of a Nation* is a 2016 American-Canadian period drama film based on the story of Nat Turner, the enslaved man who led a slave rebellion in Southampton County, Virginia, in 1831. The 2016 film uses the same title as D. W. Griffith's 1915 KKK propaganda film in a very purposeful way. Parker said his film had the same title: "ironically, but very much by design. Griffith's film relied heavily on racist propaganda to evoke fear and desperation as a tool to solidify white supremacy as the lifeblood of American sustenance. Not only did this film motivate the massive resurgence of the terror group the Ku Klux Klan and the carnage exacted against people of African descent, it served as the foundation of the film industry we know today. I've reclaimed this title and re-purposed it as a tool to challenge racism and white supremacy in America, to inspire a riotous disposition towards any and all injustice in this country (and abroad) and to promote the kind of honest confrontation that will galvanize our society towards healing and sustained systemic change." Ford, Rebecca. "'Birth of a Nation': The Slave-Revolt Movie That Will Have Sundance Talking." The *Hollywood Reporter*, January 20, 2016.

17 Stephanopoulos, George (ABC News Chief Anchor). Interview with President Trump, aired June 13, 2019.

18 Martin, Rachel (NPR). Interview with Hillary Clinton, *Morning Edition*, aired September 12, 2017.

Chapter Four

1 Seward, Theodore F. Jubilee Singers (Fisk University); "Go Down Moses." New York: Biglow & Main, 1872.

2 *Holy Bible*, New International Version, Exodus 8:1. Zondervan Publishing House, 1984.

3 Cornelius, Steven. *Music of the Civil War Era*. Portsmouth, New Hampshire: Greenwood Publishing Group, 2004, p. 118.

4 To 'go down' was to go into the dwelling of the enslaved. This could be both spiritually and physically. It is vastly different than when Moses went up to Mount Sinai to dwell with God.

5 Gandhi, Lakshmi. "What Does 'Sold Down The River' Really Mean? The Answer Isn't Pretty." NPR Code Switch: Word Watch, January 27, 2014.

6 Pogrebin, Letty. *Deborah, Golda and Me: Being Female and Jewish in America*. New York: Crown, 1991.

7 Webb, Clive. "The Nazi persecution of Jews and the African American freedom struggle." *Patterns of Prejudice*, 2019, 53:4, pp. 337–362.

8 Baldwin, James. "A Letter From A Region In My Mind." *The New Yorker*, November 10, 1962.

9 Ratskoff, Ben. "James Baldwin's Black Critique of Jewish Whiteness." *Jewish Studies Quarterly*, Vol. 27.3, 2020, pp. 240–260.

10 Berger, Roger. *Surviving the Holocaust*: A Life Course Perspective. New York: Taylor & Francis, 2010, p. 38.

11 'Tikkun olam' means to do something with the world that will not only fix any damage, but also improve upon it. 'Tikkun' is often translated as *repair*. 'Olam' connotes *all of time*. In later Hebrew, it came to mean the world. It is an opportunity to heal the world and do good. (https://www.chabad.org/library/article_cdo/aid/3700275/jewish/What-Is-Tikkun-Olam.ht)

12 Kempner, Aviva. *Rosenwald: The Remarkable Story of a Jewish Partnership with African American Communities.* Ciesla Foundation (http://rosenwaldfilm.org/rosenwald/), 2018.

13 Friedland, Michael B. *Lift Up Your Voice Like a Trumpet: White Clergy and the Civil Rights and Antiwar Movements.* Chapel Hill, North Carolina: University of North Carolina Press, 1998), pp. 77–79.

14 Quoted in Fierman, Morton C. *Leap of Action: Ideas in the Theology of Abraham Joshua Heschel.* New York: Lanham, 1990, p. 31.

15 Kandil, Caitlin Yoshiko. "Susannah Heschel on the Legacy of Her Father, Rabbi Abraham Joshua Heschel and the Civil Rights Movement." *Moment Magazine*, April 30, 2015.

16 Weinstein, Dina. "Reading Freedom Summer." Jewish Book Council, PB Daily, June 18, 2014.

17 Dixie Jubilee Singers, May 30/June 1924. Print: White, Clarence Cameron. "Forty Negro Spirituals." Philadelphia: Theodore Presser Co., 1927.

18 *The Book of Resolutions of The United Methodist Church*, Social Principles, 162H and 163F, 2016.

19 *Holy Bible*, Matthew 19:24; Mark 10:25; and Luke 18:25.

20 King Jr., Martin Luther. *Strength to Love*. Cleveland: Collins + World, 1977. In writing *Strength to Love* (first published in 1963), Dr. King drew on his preaching, which for over a decade centred on dismantling fear (for example, "Conquest of Fear," August 20, 1950 and "The Mastery of Fear," July 21, 1957). King sought, through non-violence, to bring harmony and unity to a broken society. His solution was *agape* – a love that is concerned with going the extra mile to ensure the well-being of others – for *agape* is the balm to heal a nation, and the antidote to fear. The capstone of King's efforts came when he was honoured by the Nobel Peace Prize in 1964.

21 *Torah*, Leviticus 19:34.

22 Hadith 13.

23 *Holy Bible*, Ephesians 5:1–2.

Chapter Five

1   Muddy Waters was born McKinley Morganfield sometime around 1915 in Rolling Fork, Mississippi. He was an American blues singer-songwriter and musician who was an important figure in the post-war blues scene, and is often cited as the "father of modern Chicago blues". He was raised by his grandmother, Della Grant in Clarksdale on Stovall Plantation after his mother died when he was three. He lived in a shack, working as a farm labourer from when he was a boy. Life was harsh, brutal even, with poverty and deprivation part of daily life. Take his 1959 Single Version of "Take the Bitter With The Sweet", in which he remembers the struggles and difficulties of growing up in poverty. He sings about the pain of not having any family. The song, interestingly, concludes with the line: "Oh Lord, boy I gotta take the bitter

with the sweet," which is a surprisingly upbeat and positive take on the woes that he's just been singing about.

2   Hauser, Christine; Taylor, Derrick Bryson; Vigdor, Neil. "'I Can't Breathe': 4 Minneapolis Officers Fired After Black Man Dies in Custody." *The New York Times*, May 26, 2020.

3   Brenner, Michaela; Hearing, Vincent J. "The Protective Role of Melanin Against UV Damage in Human Skin." *Photochemistry and Photobiology*, 2008, 84: 539–549.

4   "#BlackLivesMatter was founded in 2013 in response to the acquittal of Trayvon Martin's murderer. Black Lives Matter Global Network Foundation, Inc. is a global organization in the US, UK, and Canada, whose mission is to eradicate white supremacy and build local power to intervene in violence inflicted on Black communities by the state and vigilantes. By combating and countering acts of violence, creating space for Black imagination and innovation, and centering Black joy, we are winning immediate improvements in our lives." (from https://blacklivesmatter.com/about/)

5   Bunch, Lonnie G. *A Fool's Errand: Creating the National Museum of African American History and Culture During the Age of Bush, Obama, and Trump*. Washington D.C.: Smithsonian, 2019, p. 10.

6   Buell, Spencer. "Someone Beheaded the Christopher Columbus Statue in Boston...Again." *Boston Magazine*, June 10, 2020. (https://www.bostonmagazine.com/news/2020/06/10/christopher-columbus-statue-beheaded/)

7   Burford, Rachael. "Statue of 18th century slaver Robert Milligan in east London removed after pressure from campaigners." *Evening Standard* (London), June 9, 2020.

8   Calaresu, Melissa; Rubies, Joan-Pau; de Vivo, Filippo. *Exploring Cultural History: Essays in Honour of Peter Burke.* London: Routledge, 2010.

9   Duster, Michelle. *Ida in Her Own Words: The Timeless Writings of Ida B. Wells from 1893.* Lansing, Illinois: Benjamin Williams Publishing, 2008.

10 Brycchan, Carey. "William Wilberforce's Sentimental Rhetoric: Parliamentary Reportage and the Abolition Speech of 1789," *The Age of Johnson: A Scholarly Annual,* Vol. 14, 2003, pp. 281–305.

11 Doddridge, Philip. *The Rise and Progress of Religion in the Soul.* Whitefish, Montana: Kessinger, 2003 (first published 1822).

12 Brycchan, Carey. "William Wilberforce's Sentimental Rhetoric: Parliamentary Reportage and the Abolition Speech of 1789," *The Age of Johnson: A Scholarly Annual,* Vol. 14, 2003, pp. 281–305.

13 Hansard. "Slave Trade Abolition Bill," Vol. 8, cc717–22, February 10, 1807.

14 Henry, Natasha L. "Slavery Abolition Act." *Encyclopaedia Britannica,* July 25, 2020.

15 U.S. Const., Art. XII was passed by Congress on January 31, 1865, and ratified on December 6, 1865. It abolished slavery in the United States and provides that: "Neither slavery nor involuntary servitude, except as a punishment for crime whereof the party shall have been duly convicted, shall exist within the United States, or any place subject to their jurisdiction."

16 Peat, Jack. "UK Taxpayers were Paying Compensation to Slave Traders until 2015". *The London Economic,* June 11, 2020.

17 Schelzig, Erick. "Should toppled Carmack statue be repaired at Tennessee Capitol?" *The Tennessee Journal On The Hill*, June 1, 2020.

Chapter Six

1   "Respect" was originally a clever gender-bending song by Otis Redding. His intent was to reinforce the traditional family structure of the time: the man works all day, brings money home to his wife, and demands her respect in return. However, the song hit the top of the charts four months later with lead vocalist Aretha Franklin turning it into a feminist anthem, spelling out RESPECT.

2   Aretha Louise Franklin was an American singer, songwriter, actress, pianist, and Civil Rights activist, who became known as the 'Queen of Soul'. She began singing gospel as a child in Detroit, Michigan, where her father, C. L. Franklin, was a pastor. She began her secular-music career at the age of 18, with Columbia Records. Her music genius brought her enormous success and international fame.

3   Luna, Aletheia; Sol, Mateo. *Awakened Empath: The Ultimate Guide to Emotional, Psychological and Spiritual Healing*. United States: CreateSpace Independent, 2017.

4   "Make America Great Again" (MAGA) was a campaign slogan which was popularized by Donald Trump in his successful 2016 presidential bid. He revived and adapted it from a similar slogan, "Let's Make America Great Again", used by Ronald Reagan in his successful 1980 presidential bid. The terminology has long been held within American politics to be divisive. Marissa Melton reported it as a coded racism: "Is 'Make America Great Again' Racist?" *Voice of America*, August 31, 2017. Kristen Jordan Shamus described it as a symbol of hate: "MAGA hats: Trump campaign swag or symbols of hate?" Detroit Free Press, January 24, 2019. Robin

Abcarian wrote "MAGA hats and blackface are different forms of expression, but they share a certain unfortunate DNA." *Los Angeles Times*, February 5, 2019.

5   Engel Bromwich, Jonah. "Congressman Who Shouted 'You Lie' at Obama Hears the Same From Constituents." *The New York Times*, November 11, 2017.

6   The U.S. Constitution is a living document that provides guidance for America's national government and fundamental laws, and guarantees certain basic rights for its citizens. It was signed on September 17, 1787, by delegates to the Constitutional Convention in Philadelphia, which at the time was the nation's capital. Prior to its signing, the government functioned with "The Articles of Confederation", which it was believed had crafted a weak national government, allowing the original 13 states to operate like independent countries. The new document would provide for a stronger national government with three branches – executive, legislative, and judicial. The mandate created a system of checks and balances to ensure no single branch would have too much power.

7   First Reconstruction Act, U.S. The Act outlined the terms for the readmission to representation of rebel states. The bill divided the former Confederate states, except for Tennessee, into five military districts. Each state was required to write a new constitution, which needed to be approved by a majority of voters – including African Americans – in that state. In addition, each state was required to ratify the 13th and 14th Amendments to the Constitution. After meeting these criteria related to protecting the rights of African Americans and their property, the former Confederate states could gain full recognition and federal representation in Congress. The act became law on March 2, 1867, after Congress overrode a presidential veto. Admission to representation of the former

Confederate states began the next year, with Arkansas leading the way on June 22, 1868.

8   U.S. Const. Amend. XV. Grants: "The right of citizens of the United States to vote shall not be denied or abridged by the United States or by any State on account of race, color, or previous condition of servitude." It thereby granted African American men the right to vote. However, despite the 15th Amendment being passed by Congress on February 26, 1869, and ratified on February 3, 1870, discriminatory practices were used to prevent Blacks from exercising their right to vote. It wasn't until the Voting Rights Act of 1965 that legal barriers that were still being used, at the state and local levels, to deny African Americans their right to vote under the 15th Amendment were resolved and fully outlawed under the constitution.

9   Ginzburg, Ralph. "Perth Amboy Church is 302 and Counting." *The New York Times*, February 15, 1987.

10   U.S. Const. Amend. XIV. After the Civil War, Congress submitted to the states three amendments as part of its Reconstruction programme to guarantee equal civil and legal rights to Black citizens. The first section of the 14th Amendment is often deemed the most significant; it granted citizenship "to all persons born or naturalized in the United States—including former slaves," and guaranteed all citizens equal protection under the law. The Amendment was passed by Congress on June 13, 1866, and ratified on July 9, 1868.

11   Jim Crow laws were designed to enforce racial segregation in the southern U.S. states. These laws lasted from the end of the Reconstruction period in 1877 until the implementation of the Civil Rights Act of 1964. The name 'Jim Crow' was based on a minstrel routine (actually called 'Jump Jim Crow') that was performed by its author, Thomas Dartmouth ("Daddy") Rice.

12 Budiman, Abby. "Key facts about Black eligible voters in 2020 battleground states." *Fact Tank*, October 21, 2020.

13 Griffin, Robert; Frey, William H.; Teixeira, Ruy. "States of Change: Demographic Change, Representation Gaps, and Challenges to Democracy, 1980–2060." Center for American Progress, February, 2017.

14 This data was calculated with a series of studies to determine the percentage. There was no clear evidence. Included in the data collection were reports from the 2018 U.S. Census Bureau, CNN Exit Poll, Pew Research Center, and The Brookings Institute.

15 Du Bois, W.E.B. *The Souls of Black Folk*, "Of the Sons of Master and Man." Chicago: A.C. McClurg & Co., 1903, Chapter 9, p. 10.

16 Ibid Du Bois, Chapter 9, p. 10.

17 H.R.3355 – Violent Crime Control and Law Enforcement Act of 1994, 103rd Congress (1993–1994). This is the largest crime bill in the history of the U.S. and provided for 100,000 new police officers, $9.7 billion in funding for prisons, and $6.1 billion in funding for prevention programmes, which were designed with significant input from experienced police officers. The Crime Bill provided $2.6 billion in additional funding for the Federal Bureau of Investigation (FBI), Drug Enforcement Agency (DEA), Immigration and Naturalization Service (INS), United States Attorneys, and other Justice Department components, as well as the Federal courts and the Treasury Department.

18 Kessler, Gleen. "Joe Biden's defense of the 1994 crime bill's role in mass incarcerations." *The Washington Post*, May 16, 2019.

19 Uggen, Chris; Larson, Ryan; Shannon, Sarah; Pullido-Nava, Arleth. "Locked Out 2020: Estimates of People Denied Voting Rights Due to a Felony Conviction." The Sentencing Project, October 30, 2020.

Chapter Six

1   McCall, David; Ahrens, Lynn. "*Schoolhouse Rock!*: The Preamble." New York: Scholastic Rock, Inc., ABC, 1974.

2   Soul Train is an American music television show that prominently featured African American musical acts and dancers. It was the brainchild of a local Chicago radio announcer Don Cornelius and broadcast nationally from 1971 to 2006. It provided a national and international lens into Black culture revealing it as upbeat, exciting, and vibrant, attracting a viewing audience of other ethnicities. It is noted as having made a significant contribution to elevating the prestige of African Americans and of Black culture in the mainstream.

3   Gamble, Kenny; Huff, Leon. "The Sound of Philadelphia (*Soul Train* theme song)." Philadelphia: Philadelphia International Records, 1973.

4   *Schoolhouse Rock!* is U.S. television series of animated, musical, educational short films (and later, videos) that aired during the Saturday morning children's programming on ABC. The themes covered included grammar, science, economics, history, mathematics, and civics. The series aired from 1973 to 1984 and it was later revived, adding new episodes from 1993 to 1996.

5   McCall, David; Ahrens, Lynn. "*Schoolhouse Rock!*: The Preamble." New York: Scholastic Rock, Inc., ABC, 1974.

6   Frederick Douglass was born into slavery sometime around 1818 in Talbot County, Maryland. He was one of the most profound intellectuals of his time. His writing *Narrative of the Life of Frederick Douglass, an American Slave*, describes his life experiences, including being a slave, life after the Civil War, and a tour of Britain to garner support for the abolition of slavery in the U.S.

7   Susan B. Anthony was an American abolitionist and writer, who was a leading figure in the women's voting rights movement. She was raised in a Quaker family in Rochester, New York. Her family became deeply involved in the fight to end slavery, the abolitionist movement. After partnering with Elizabeth Cady Stanton, she would eventually lead the National American Woman Suffrage Association.

8   First Reconstruction Act, U.S., Sec. 5.: "And be it further enacted, That when the people of any one of said rebel States shall have formed a constitution of government in conformity with the Constitution of the United States in all respects, framed by a convention of delegates elected by the male citizens of said State, twenty-one years old and upward, of whatever race, color, or previous condition, who have been resident in said State for one year previous to the day of such election, except such as may be disfranchised for participation in the rebellion or for felony at common law, and when such constitution shall provide that the elective franchise shall be enjoyed by all persons as have the qualifications herein states for electors of delegates, and when such constitution shall be ratified by a majority of the persons voting on the question of ratification who are qualified as electors for delegates, and when such constitution shall have been submitted to Congress for examination and approval, and Congress shall have approved the same, and when said State, by a vote of its legislature elected under said constitution, shall have

adopted the amendment to the Constitution of the United States, proposed by the Thirty-ninth Congress, and known as article fourteen and when said article shall have become a part of the Constitution of the United States said State shall be declared entitled to representation in Congress, and senators and representatives shall be admitted therefrom on their taking the oath prescribed by law, and then and thereafter the preceding sections of this act shall be inoperative in said State: Provided, That no person excluded from the privilege of holding office by said proposed amendment to the Constitution of the United States, shall be eligible to election as a member of the convention to frame a constitution for any of said rebel States, nor shall any person vote for members of such convention."

9   Isabella Baumfree was the given name of the notable Sojourner Truth, who was an American abolitionist and women's rights activist. She was born into slavery in Swartekill, New York. She is best-known for her sermon, or speech, known as '*Ain't I a Woman?*' It was delivered in 1851 at the Ohio Women's Rights Convention in Akron, Ohio. Her name change to *Sojourner Truth* was because, she said, "The (Holy) Spirit calls me, and I must go." She became a Methodist and left to make her way traveling and preaching about abolition. ('Amazing Life' page, *Sojourner Truth Institute site,* retrieved September 12, 2019). She published *The Narrative of Sojourner Truth: A Northern Slave* (1850), Dover Publications 1997, that chronicle her journey from slavery to freedom, as a wife, mother, itinerant preacher and activist.

10 Truth, Sojourner. "Ain't I A Woman?" (Penguin Great Ideas). New York: Penguin, 2020.

11 Women's Rights Convention, Sojourner Truth, *Anti-Slavery Bugle*, June 21, 1851, p. 160, Public Domain.

12 Washington, Booker T.; Du Bois, W.E.B. (et al). "The Negro Problem: The Talented Tenth." New York: J. Pott & Company, 1903.

13 Du Bois, W. E. B. *The Souls of Black Folk*. New York: New American Library, Inc, 1903, pp. 10, 29.

14 Du Bois, W. E. B. *The Souls of Black Folk*, New York: New American Library, Inc, 1903, pp. 10–11.

15 The Editors of *Encyclopædia Britannica*. "Themis." *Encyclopædia Britannica*, February 7, 2018; https://www.britannica.com/topic/Themis-Greek-goddess, November 30, 2020.

16 King Jr., Martin Luther. Sermon: "The Mastery of Fear." Montgomery, Alabama: July 21, 1957.

17 Socrates asserts that justice sustains and perfects the other three cardinal virtues: Temperance, Wisdom, and Courage. He argues that justice is the cause and condition of their very existence. He does not include justice as a virtue within the city but rather indicates that justice does not exist within the human soul either. He believes that justice is a result of a "well-ordered" soul. *Plato's The Republic*. New York: Books, Inc., 1943. Cornford, Francis; Hildebrandt, Kurt; and Voegelin, Eric: contribution to an establishment of subdivisions marked by special formulae in Greek, *Organization of the Republic*, Part I: "Genesis and Order of the Polis," IV.6–IV.19. 427c–445e. "Justice in the Polis."

18 Donald Cornelius was the host of the nationally syndicated dance and music show *Soul Train*, from 1971 until 1993. Known for his smooth and deep baritone voice, and his afro, notably he concluded the show with the catchphrase "I'm Don Cornelius, and as always in parting, we wish you love, peace and soul!" He was speaking to give each viewer a sense of hope.

The Afterthought

1   From "My Country 'Tis of Thee" by Samuel F. Smith, 1831.

2   From "Lift Every Voice and Sing" by James Weldon Johnson, 1900.

3   *Holy Bible*, New International Version, Amos 5:24. Zondervan Publishing House, 1984.

4   *Holy Bible,* New International Version, Micah 6:8. Zondervan Publishing House, 1984.

5   *Holy Bible*, New International Version, 1 John 4:18. Zondervan Publishing House, 1984.

CPSIA information can be obtained
at www.ICGtesting.com
Printed in the USA
LVHW080238150221
679322LV00021B/856/J